RETAIL SELLING
— Everyone's Business

How to Achieve Maximum Retail Sales

Peter Fleming

2000

First published in 1995 by
Management Books 2000 Ltd,
Cowcombe House,
Cowcombe Hill,
Chalford,
Gloucestershire GL6 8HP
United Kingdom
Tel: 01285-760722
Fax: 01285-760708

Reprinted 1996, 2000

Printed and bound in Great Britain by Biddles, Guidford

British Library Cataloguing in Publication Data is available

ISBN 1-85252-295-X

RETAIL SELLING

LEARNING
SUPPORT
SERVICES

Please return
on or before
the last date
stamped below

City College
NORWICH

15. MAY 2003

14. OCT. 2003

1 9 JUL 2004

0 3 NOV 2004

1 2 JAN 2005

2 5 NOV 2005

2 1 NOV 2006

1 0 APR 2008

- 8 OCT 2010

1 0 MAY 2016

195 032

BSSA Guides for Retailers

This book is part of a new series of specialist guide books for retailers, edited by Peter Fleming, of PFA Business and Personnel Development Consultants. The series deals with topical issues in retailing today, covering such areas as sales techniques (this book), retail management, law for retailers, buying techniques, the retailer and the community, and others to be determined.

Each book is practical, with checklists, action plans and, where appropriate, personal assignments. Each publication relates to others in the series. Closely based on good practice in the industry, the books are designed to help individuals to improve their performance at work, achieve greater satisfaction from their jobs and contribute to better company performance. For further information, or to order other books in the series, telephone Management Books 2000 on 01285-760722.

BSSA

The British Shops and Stores Association (BSSA) plays an important part both in influencing and reflecting the views of the retail industry, with a brief to serve, protect and advance the interests of non-food retailers. In practical terms that means lobbying both UK and European legislators on a wide range of issues which affect specialist retailers; offering impartial advice on legal, financial and property matters and providing a helpline for day to day business problems.

The Association's training mission is

• to enable retailing firms achieve productivity, profitability and excellence in customer service through their investment in people;

• to promote and provide the means by which people at all levels in distribution can develop their skills to the limits of their aspirations.

BSSA's commitment to its members does not stop at good advice. With particular expertise in the fields of ladies' and men's fashions, fabrics, general merchandise, furniture, furnishings and carpets, a range of commercial and other services are regularly evaluated and updated. Whether there is a need to increase efficiency and commitment through training, insure the business via BSSA's broking services or save time and money when making regular payments, BSSA has retailers' interests constantly in mind.

Operating in dynamic trading environments, influenced by political, economic, social and technological pressures, retailers today have to respond to constant change. To stay ahead they need timely, accurate and unbiased advice – and BSSA is the first source that many turn to!

Full details of membership and further information on the Association is available from Middleton House, 2 Main Road, Middleton Cheney, Banbury, Oxon. OX17 2TN (telephone 01295-712277 or facsimile 01295-711665).

Preface

There are two main requirements for a successful business – a thumping good idea and a really enthusiastic sales force to go out and sell it! Retail sales people provide vital services to the community and the tourist industry, and this book – it's really a manual – gives the sales person a great opportunity to develop key skills which will help them achieve success in this crucial job. I have no hesitation in recommending it to you.

Tim Daniels
Managing Director
Selfridges Ltd

Introduction

Welcome to the first in what will be a series of books written specifically for retailers and service sector businesses. There are many books in print about aspects of selling technique – but not many of them have been specifically targeted towards retailers and their staff. So, why should *you* read this book?

Sadly, many people learn their selling skills the hard way – by trial and error! The trouble with this is that it can be an expensive way to learn – lost sales, complaints, cancelled orders, even a polite suggestion from your manager that "perhaps you are not really suited to this job in selling" might result from this learning method!

Some of the ideas in this book may be known to some readers; if you feel this applies to you, perhaps you should ask yourself:

- Do I try to put this idea or technique into practice?
- All the time? Some of the time? Ever?
- Can I make it work? If not, why?

So, as you read, you should be challenging yourself: "Did I know that? Have I tried it? Did it work and, if not, how could I be more successful?" Participants on our public training courses are quick to recognise when a technique is useful and when it does not fit their own personal selling style. Selling is as much about personality and personal style as it is about skills and techniques and will be effective only when you are comfortable with the techniques you use.

The ultimate judge of your selling skills is your customer – and your sales achievements will prove just how successful you are in your everyday task. To enhance your application of the skills here, you should try to obtain some direct feedback on your performance and methods. One way of doing this would be to attend a training workshop which includes some role-play exercises and video feedback. There is no finer way of improving your selling skills in such a "safe" environment. We will be very pleased to offer enquirers a training method which will achieve this on an in-company basis.

Finally, selling can be a fascinating occupation – both challenging and frustrating at times, but rarely boring! I hope that you find this book makes a major contribution to a highly successful sales career and look forward to meeting you, perhaps, on a training course in the future.

Peter Fleming
PFA Business & Personnel Development
Bay Tree House, Sutton Wick Lane,
Drayton, Abingdon, Oxon OX14 4HJ
Tel./Fax: 01235 – 534124

CONTENTS

1

Who Am I?

"I have an outgoing personality, I try to project warm and friendly feelings and feel quite comfortable about leading customers towards the purchases which will best fit their needs."

1. Introduction

"So, you are interested in a career in selling, are you? What makes you think you can make a career out of that? Why not try something more reliable – like working for a bank, or a building society?"

Have you heard that said before? Perhaps you have even said it to members of your family – and, in doing so, have unwittingly perpetuated the myth that somehow selling is not a particularly worthy occupation.

The plain truth is that, in every business, everyone needs to be a seller – and to be good at it. Yes, everyone from the switchboard operator to the delivery driver, finance director to the cash desk staff, central buyer to the merchandiser – all need to help drive the business forward. This may not mean that everyone actually sells merchandise, but it does mean that there will be occasions when they all sell ideas and concentrate on putting the customer's needs first.

The process will be easier if they show their:

- Concern for customers' needs
- Enthusiastic support of the business's merchandise and sales methods
- Wish to see the business prosper and grow

- Cheerfulness in everyday contact with colleagues, staff and customers.

How does this all apply to you? Are you a person who has an outgoing personality, is enthusiastic, and positive about life? If not, could you be such a person, capable of concentrating on the "optimistic" side of things? If so, you start with an in-built advantage.

In this first chapter, we are going to look at ourselves:

- Our personal qualities – especially our strengths and weaknesses
- The aspects of our personality which will make it easier to sell success-fully
- Our starting knowledge
- An overview of the skills we need to develop.

And here is the first key learning point:

 There are no single, fixed approaches to selling that will always bring 100 per cent success. There are, however, techniques which mark out the difference between average and skilled salespeople and we are going to explore these in our Key Learning Points.

To put it another way, failure to follow the advice contained in this book will not automatically doom you to failure! Equally, unless you have a unique instinct for selling, the guidance in this book should help you avoid the common pitfalls and achieve greater success.

Why is this? Because we are describing skills which are valuable in dealing with people and everyone is different. Approaches which will work perfectly satisfactorily with one customer may seem to "turn off" another. This irritating fact actually provides the key to what makes any customer contact role so fascinating. We really have to become a bit of a psychologist.

2. Personal Skills

So, what are the qualities that are likely to help us achieve success? We are going to follow a simple framework, adding up to a powerful memory-jogger:

P – E – R – S – O – N – A – L   S – K – I – L – L – S

P = Presentation with confidence

Dealing with the public can often feel a little like being on a stage. Customers expect service assistants to know what they are talking about and, with good knowledge, our confidence level will improve. (In contrast, absence of an adequate level of knowledge is likely to make the sales person diffident at best – and positively stand-offish at worst.) This could explain why some sales people seem reluctant to approach customers: they are worried they might be asked a question which they cannot handle.

The process of selling involves imparting or presenting information to customers in such a way as to encourage them to make the purchase, return again in the future and continue to deal with your firm. In later sections we will consider ways in which we can enhance our presentations to make them even more persuasive. For the moment, you could begin by assessing your present level of confidence. Is it as good as your colleagues – not as good – or better?

Even when we have a good level of knowledge there are still pitfalls to avoid. In-depth knowledge can lead to overconfidence and even cockiness. Customers may be quickly put off by the "clever" sales person.

 Key Learning Point: Sales people need confidence. This confidence is based on sound retailing and product knowledge.

E = Empathy in meeting and greeting strangers

Empathy is a way of describing our ability to get on the same "wavelength" as the customer and to establish a constructive relationship – quickly. The best way of achieving this is by presenting a warm, friendly image – building good eye contact, smiling and being prepared to listen to the customer. All rather obvious points! However, this is not always as easy as it sounds. Have you ever had to keep smiling for a length of time – say, for a photograph? You were very lucky if your face muscles did not hurt after a while (unless your normal expression is to smile!). A constant passage of customers by your cash desk, counter or work station can be exhausting for most of us – even when we really like people. So, consider what it can be like for the person who finds people tiresome or unnerving. Customers do not know what kind of day you have been experiencing – they expect you to be as fresh at 5.30 pm or 8 pm as you might have been at 9 am.

We all have a "body-clock" and our ability to cope with the pressures of business can be affected by our clock. Some people are best in the morning – they have sometimes been called "larks". Others are "night-owls" and are at their best after lunch or in the evening. The way our body-clock works can affect our levels of:

- Patience
- Concentration
- Energy
- Enthusiasm

and, if these resources are low, customers will often detect it. How can you control these factors? First of all, your physical health will play a part. If you are constantly tired, your empathy and enthusiasm level will probably suffer. So, if you are working the next day – don't go to bed too late! Also, your energy levels will be affected by your eating habits. Customer service requires concentration and alertness – so it is demanding on our brainpower. You will find that your ability to concentrate on customers' needs may decline during the day and will only be refreshed by work-breaks. It is a mistake not to take a break at "coffee" or "tea" time and it is also a good idea to take your full lunch break and get away from your normal workplace for a while. You will feel refreshed – even if you only browse around a competitor's business.

 Key Learning Point: Customers do not know what kind of day you have been experiencing. They expect you to be as fresh at 5.30 pm or 8 pm as you might have been at 9 am.

R = Resilience in handling rejection

Most natural sales people have a personality which could be described as extrovert; we enjoy meeting people and warm to the challenge of trying to influence their purchasing decisions. However, the job can also involve a great deal of rejection. This can come from:

- Customers who are resistant to being persuaded into a purchase they had not intended to make
- Customers who do not have the same kind of extrovert personality as the sales person and may therefore seem rather "cold"
- Customers who are low reactors – they just do not talk very much
- Ill-mannered people.

The fact is that all of these types of people could easily become customers – and that is our aim. So we have to be able to rise above the negative vibes which we may feel in suffering rejection from these customers.

Here are some examples of what can happen:

Example 1

Customer walks past the service desk or greeting point...

Assistant: "Good afternoon."

Customer ignores the greeting and walks right past to look at something at the far end of the shop or restaurant...

Assistant thinks: "Blow you then! I'll just wait until you need some help – and then you will have to come back to me."

An understandable reaction – but wrong! Customers are guests in your business and, right or wrong, polite or rude, must be treated with respect and politeness (even if this is not forthcoming from them).

Example 2

Assistant: "Hello, can I help you?"

Customer: "No thank you, I'm just looking."

Assistant thinks: "Just like thousands of others I've met today. A waste of time!"

Another negative reaction; but don't sales persons who use this approach bring the rejection on themselves? (We will discuss different customer approaches and greetings later.) As we will learn later, many customers need to have a look at your range or offers before they can assess what they like or dislike. Our task is to offer advice or help just when they need it. How many times have you been able to turn a browser into a customer? A really successful sales person would answer "most of the time" – but this will not happen with a negative attitude.

Example 3

Tracy is a switchboard operator ...

Operator: "Thank you for calling Blands of Westhampton, Tracy speaking, how may I help you?"

Caller: "Mr Jenkins."

Operator thinks:"Please and thank you would not go amiss. Why should I knock myself out? You won't catch me bowing and scraping to these people. It'll serve him right if Fred Jenkins is not there. I'll just switch the customer through." – click!

Once again, this was not a positive exchange. It would be tempting to become greasily polite in the face of such abruptness but retaliation is no way to treat a caller who may turn out to be the firm's best customer or most important supplier.

 Key Learning Point: We have a right to be treated with respect in life but selling is all about creating a working relationship with the customer and rising above any negative feelings.

Before we move on, stop and do this assignment:

Assignment 1. Handling rejection

In the above three examples write in the exchange you would make to the customer/caller.

When you have completed this assignment, check the model answers in Appendix 2.

Example 1

Customer walks past the service desk or greeting point...

Assistant: "Good afternoon"

Customer ignores the greeting and walks right past to look at something at the far end of the shop or restaurant.

Your answer:

✍ ....

....

....

Example 2:

Assistant: "Hello, can I help you?"

Customer: "No thank you, I'm just looking."

Your answer:

✍ ....

....

....

Example 3

Tracy is a switchboard operator ....

Operator: "Thank you for calling Blands of Westhampton, Tracy speaking, how may I help you?"

Caller: "Mr Jenkins."

Your answer:

✍ ....

....

....

S = Sincerity

When we are trying to influence other people it is very tempting to put on an act – to become something of an entertainer, or perhaps to adopt a quick-fire way of speaking which might be similar to the methods used by street vendors. Customers can quickly distinguish between "sales chat" and sincere advice. How can they tell? It could be through:

- Tone of voice – not too brash
- An open manner – good, positive eye contact
- Careful use of posture and gesture – open hand movements (but not too many of them)
- Avoidance of catchphrases – as used by popular comedians
- Ability to "talk from the heart".

 Key Learning Point: A sincere sales person will always appear to speak with the best interests of the customer in mind – neither too "pushy" nor economical with the truth.

O = Open questions

An important quality (or skill) is that of being able to ask questions of your customers. This implies not only being able to keep quiet long enough to give the customer a chance to speak, but also listening to the answers! Questions can lead us down a cul-de-sac if we are not careful (remember the greeting example 3 above?). "Can I help you" is a closed question – it is likely to lead to the response "Yes" or "No".

 Key Learning Point: Open questions are much better to use. Try using – "How may I help you?"

N = Normally overcoming objections

Objections occur in most sales persons' daily lives. Not every customer or client will readily accept everything we might say about the merchandise or service we have to offer.

Comments like:

- "I don't like the colour" or
- "That is too expensive"

may seem like an insurmountable roadblock – but effective sales people just see them as a hurdle to jump *with* the customer rather than an impossible barrier which could lead to the loss of the sale.

How do you see objections? Do you work hard to overcome them, with a positive attitude, or are they yet another tiresome factor contributing to the overall stress of the salesperson's life?

 Key Learning Point: Objections are quite normal and do not spell disaster for the sale.

A = Answering questions honestly

Have you ever met someone who never seemed to answer your questions or avoided them, leaving you with an uncomfortable feeling that they either did not know the answer to your question or preferred you not to know the answer? Would you want to do business with them again? Probably not. This does not mean that you always have to give the customer the blunt truth in such a way that it puts them off buying the product. For example:

19

Customer: "How do you think I look in this jacket?"

Assistant: "To be truthful, it has enough room in it for two of you!"

Perhaps the customer is deliberately seeking the loose, casual look, in which case the assistant might have said:

"Well, it will be ideal for using on the golf course – as you were telling me you play quite a lot. There is plenty of room in it to allow you complete freedom of movement. Just what you need for a good swing!"

 Key Learning Point: Selling is about presenting ideas and information in a positive light.

L = Looking for buying signals

Skilled sales people know when to stop talking and close the sale. They are sensitive to customers' moods, attitudes and reactions – and the subtle shifts in body language which say "I want to buy this – don't say any more."

Insensitive or less skilled people keep babbling on about the product or service and risk talking themselves out of the sale altogether. Hasn't this happened to you as a customer at some time? You have really wanted to say: "Please shut up ... I give in ... I want to buy it ..." (We will look at buying signals in detail in a later chapter.)

 Key Learning Point: Buying signals can save you a lot of effort if you read them correctly.

S = Selection of the product or service

There is a bewildering selection of goods and services available in a sophisticated country such as ours and, for uninitiated customers, it is easy to see why some are simply confused by choice. The fact is that many people need professional guidance in order to make the right choice – whether this is a suitable cocktail dress, a durable carpet, a flexible payment plan or a low calorie meal.

Key Learning Point: Our aim, as professional sales people, should be to sell the right product or service to meet the needs of the customer. This means finding out about those needs first.

K = Knowledge of products

All this is easier if the sales person has detailed knowledge of the portfolio of products and services available in today's menu, this season's collection or the latest model range. You can never have too much knowledge about your range of products or services; the secret lies in how to use that knowledge. We will return to this theme again later, but for the time being here is another Key Learning Point:

 The skilled sales person concentrates on what the product will do for the customer rather than on esoteric values which are of interest only to the experts.

I = Integrity

Another word for integrity is 'trust' – and customers need to feel that they can trust their sales person or customer adviser. This grows in importance with the value of the purchase and also with the extent of the customer's dependence on the assistant. If customers need technical information to help with their decision, the extent of the person's trust in the advice will affect that decision.

Many customers have a secret and inherent mistrust of sales people. They half expect that the sales person will exert too much influence and that they will be talked into a decision they will subsequently regret. Sometimes it is possible to read the customer's mind: "I must be alert here or I will be stitched up!" Persuading customers that they can relax and that the purchase selection will be easy, reliable and even enjoyable is not always as easy as it sounds.

So, the customer service process needs to be carried out with professionalism and care. It is important that the customer can detect that the "assistant" is acting with a concern for honesty. But whoever sold anything by being totally truthful? "Will this lambswool jumper wear well?" you may be asked. You are hardly likely to sell it if you say "No". However, a careful comparison between the softness of the lambswool article and the harsher Shetland will enable the assistant to help the customer choose between wearability and comfort. If your business is concerned about repeat purchases and building goodwill, it will want you to work with integrity.

 Key Learning Point: Skilled sales people always try to generate trust.

L = Listening skills

We have already seen that the sales person will find the task much easier if he or she asks customers relevant questions and encourages them to partici-pate in the sales interview. Many customers know exactly what they want; but others need help, advice and encouragement.

One of the hardest lessons to learn is not to keep talking like a person with verbal diarrhoea! There is something of the "babbler" in all sales people – but this quality definitely needs to be kept under control. How good a listener are you?

 Key Learning Point: Successful sales people know when to talk and when to listen to their customers – and manage to achieve a balance between the two.

L = Leading to a close

However much time and effort is invested in greeting customers, finding out about their needs and presenting merchandise and information to them, the whole process is purely speculative unless it results in a sale. This does not mean that the assistant should grasp every prospective customer by the lapels and demand to know: "Are you really keen to buy today or perhaps you intend to choose something in time for the millennium?" This approach would of course be unacceptable. The patient approach will usually pay dividends – and the customer could even end up buying something quite different from their original intentions. We have all bought products on an impulse and customers will often decide to buy your product or service in this way. Our job is to lead the customer round to the purchasing decision and close the sale. We will look at some specific ways of doing this later.

 Key Learning Point: Closing the sale is your main function and is best achieved by focusing on the customer's needs. This will help you steer the customer to the "finishing line".

S = Selling up and selling on

Our last quality covers these twin factors which are used to describe the selling of the better item and encouraging the customer to buy other items which are related to the first purchase. Most of us at some time or another have made a purchase decision based on a low price – only to regret not having chosen a better quality item at the time. Many customers can be persuaded to spend "that little bit more" when they are convinced that it is in their best interest to do so (the sales person has "sold up", or sold the better item). Apart from the extra value gained by the customer, your firm also gains by increasing the value of the sale (and probably the profit as well).

Similar benefits are to be gained from "selling on", or introducing related purchases before the customer has closed the sale. Suggesting a new tie to go with the shirt, a handbag to go with the shoes, "Guardsman" finish to protect the fabric on the new three-piece suite or a liqueur to go with the coffee might sound cheeky to some people, but is often accepted as an extra service by the customer. The new outfit could be really let down by last season's accessory. *You* know that; but can you convince the customer?

Case History

Sharpe & Fisher is a regional builders' merchant company with 22 branches based in the South and the South-West. Its sales teams include counter sales and sales office staff and an effective field sales force. Through the recession their sales and profits have grown against stiff competition and a shrinking construction market.

A group of branch managers on a recent sales management course were asked to identify the differences between "order takers" (i.e. those who *passively* wait for customers to make their own buying decisions and then pay the account) and true sales people who *actively* create customer satisfaction through professional selling. They arrived at the following contrasting statement of skills for the two different selling roles:

Order takers are:	*Professional sellers are:*
Followers	High achievers
Poor under stress	Assertive
Luke-warm about targets	Committed to targets
Resistant to change	Enthusiastic about new ideas
Conditioned to sell on price	Trained to sell on quality, service and then price
"Plodders" who need leadership	Interested, interesting, and self-motivated
More talkative	Better listeners
Not creative – make fewer related sales	Confident about introducing related lines
Indecisive	Quick thinkers
"Boring"	Ambitious
"Laid-back"	Users of their bright personalities in selling
Set in their ways	Good supporters and users of training ideas
Relaxed about work rate	Seekers of ways of increasing their work-rate/sales output
Slow to learn product knowledge	Apply thorough product knowledge in selling benefits

Key Learning Point: The skilled salesperson will be able to persuade the customer of the case for buying the better item and *the related accessories!*

These managers have considerable experience of selecting, managing and coaching salespeople and their meeting was designed to help them share experiences of successful sales teams and to build action plans to increase their existing successes. The meeting concluded that some of the characteristics of "professional sellers" are in-born traits but many listed in the above chart are capable of being learned and improved through personal effort and good training. Which category of sales person would you rather be known as by *your* manager?

Assignment 2

Now that we have examined the personal skills in detail try the following assignment and test yourself against the criteria listed. When you have completed the exercise turn to the end of the chapter for some further advice.

Inventory of personal skills

Please circle the score which reflects your current skill level – perhaps measured against a colleague whose skills and experience are superior or inferior to yours. Then place a cross against the score which represents your target skill level. Score 1 = Undeveloped; Score 5 = Highly developed.

Presenting confidently	1	2	3	4	5
Empathy	1	2	3	4	5
Resilience in handling rejection	1	2	3	4	5
Sincerity	1	2	3	4	5
Open questions	1	2	3	4	5
Normally overcoming objections	1	2	3	4	5
Answering questions	1	2	3	4	5
Looking for buying signals	1	2	3	4	5
Selection – helping the customer choose	1	2	3	4	5
Knowledge of products	1	2	3	4	5
Integrity	1	2	3	4	5
Listening skills	1	2	3	4	5
Leading to a close	1	2	3	4	5
Selling up and selling on	1	2	3	4	5

Case History

May's Carpets is a leading regional floor covering retailer which built its early business on aggressive pricing and good value for money, achieved by bulk buying of carpet. Pioneering the provision of a cash-and-carry approach to carpets, the business has been successful in making a move in its market position towards a "fitting and service-oriented business".

"In addition to selling carpet on a cash-and-carry basis we have decided to increase the selling skills and product knowledge of our sales and warehouse staff so that we can provide a better service to our customers," said Operations Director, Richard May. Richard reviewed his recruitment profile and decided that, as vacancies occurred, it would be more effective to recruit new staff with a sales personality and teach them about carpets, rather than to look for staff who might know something about carpets but needed to gain an ability to sell. "This is not to say that we do not train them. But we need people with 'bubbly' personalities and that is not a quality which is easy to develop in every applicant." Judging from the stream of satisfied customers leaving the store with rolls of carpet, the policy is paying off!

---

3. Review

Retailers normally see the role of sales people as:

• Meeting, greeting and concluding sales with customers who are so satisfied that they want to return in the future.

This objective can be best achieved by:

• Selling yourself
• Selling the company, and
• Selling the product.

Most sales interviews contain an element of each of these functions.

This first chapter should have helped you identify how to improve your skills in selling yourself. Later chapters will enable you to identify ways of fulfilling the other functions. We have seen in this chapter that successful sales people generally have:

• An extrovert personality

- An empathy for people
- An ability to cope with rejection
- And an ability to persuade other people to do things.

While innate qualities will help the new entrant to be successful, there are also a number of core personal skills which need to be developed – and this chapter has identified them for you.

4. Tailpiece

Under our chapter heading we quoted the salesperson's personality in terms of warmth, friendliness and leadership.. The most successful salespeople are those who are able to reveal these aspects of their personality and use them to help customers make the most effective purchases for their needs:

"I have an outgoing personality, I try to project warm and friendly feelings and feel quite comfortable about leading customers towards the purchases which will best fit their needs."

How would you describe your personality? In these terms or not? If this is not you – don't panic.

It is possible to work at presenting yourself in this way. It may not come easily at first and you may find it exhausting – but your efforts will be rewarded. If you are ready to find out more about how to use this selling style with customers – please move on to the next chapter.

5. Questionnaire

Now try our multi-choice questionnaire, which deals with issues related to Chapter 1. Please put each statement in rank order, i.e.

1 = Statement you feel to be *most* important/correct,
4 = Statement you feel to be *least* important/correct.

The correct marking scale is shown in Appendix 2 (page 179)

	1	2	3	4
1. A successful salesperson should always be:				
(a) professional, polite and friendly	☐	☐	☐	☐
(b) entertaining in conversation	☐	☐	☐	☐
(c) patient	☐	☐	☐	☐
(d) well dressed and tidy	☐	☐	☐	☐

	1	2	3	4

2. Selling skills could be described as:
   (a) an aptitude with which people are born ☐ ☐ ☐ ☐
   (b) based on product knowledge ☐ ☐ ☐ ☐
   (c) simply a matter of "getting on" with people ☐ ☐ ☐ ☐
   (d) skills which can be learned ☐ ☐ ☐ ☐

3. Success in selling lies in:
   (a) achieving high sales by being "pushy" ☐ ☐ ☐ ☐
   (b) satisfying customer needs ☐ ☐ ☐ ☐
   (c) "chatting up" the customer ☐ ☐ ☐ ☐
   (d) dazzling the customer with words or flattery ☐ ☐ ☐ ☐

4. The sales person is employed to:
   (a) keep the customer happy ☐ ☐ ☐ ☐
   (b) keep the stock moving ☐ ☐ ☐ ☐
   (c) make the customer feel "better off" with the purchase ☐ ☐ ☐ ☐
   (d) help the customer feel totally relaxed and friendly ☐ ☐ ☐ ☐

5. Having the right approach to customers:
   (a) is the basis of a joint relationship with all customers ☐ ☐ ☐ ☐
   (b) means putting manners before commission ☐ ☐ ☐ ☐
   (c) means making customers feel at home ☐ ☐ ☐ ☐
   (d) means being enthusiastic and optimistic at all times ☐ ☐ ☐ ☐

6. All sales people should:
   (a) carefully consider the effect they have on others ☐ ☐ ☐ ☐
   (b) ask themselves what effect they have on customers ☐ ☐ ☐ ☐
   (c) concentrate on "being themselves" ☐ ☐ ☐ ☐
   (d) concentrate on getting on with their colleagues ☐ ☐ ☐ ☐

7. Eye contact with customers is a:
   (a) matter of good manners ☐ ☐ ☐ ☐
   (b) a sign of being relaxed ☐ ☐ ☐ ☐
   (c) means of projecting enthusiasm for the job ☐ ☐ ☐ ☐
   (d) demonstration of honesty or sincerity ☐ ☐ ☐ ☐

8. The essence of the task of selling is:
   (a) being pleasant to customers so they "help themselves" ☐ ☐ ☐ ☐
   (b) persuading customers to buy the firm's merchandise ☐ ☐ ☐ ☐
   (c) ensuring you have the right stock to sell ☐ ☐ ☐ ☐
   (d) displaying new products as soon as they arrive. ☐ ☐ ☐ ☐

Now check your answers with the model answers in Appendix 2.

Summary of Key Learning Points

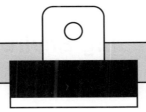

1. There are no single, fixed approaches to selling that will always bring 100 per cent success. There are, however, techniques which mark out the difference between average and skilled salespeople and we are going to explore these in our Key Learning Points.

2. Sales people need confidence. This confidence is based on sound retailing and product knowledge.

3. Customers do not know what kind of day you have been experiencing. They expect you to be as fresh at 5.30 pm or 8 pm as you might have been at 9 am.

4. We have a right to be treated with respect in life but selling is all about creating a working relationship with the customer and rising above any negative feelings.

5. A sincere sales person will always appear to speak with the best interests of the customer in mind – neither too "pushy" nor economical with the truth.

6. Open questions are much better than closed questions. Try using – "How may I help you?"

7. Objections are quite normal and do not spell disaster for the sale.

8. Selling is about presenting ideas and information in a positive light.

9. Buying signals can save you a lot of effort if you "read" them correctly.

10. Our aim, as professional sales people, should be to sell the right product or service to meet the needs of the customer. This means finding out about those needs first.

11. The skilled sales person concentrates on what the product will do for the customer rather than on esoteric values which are of interest only to the experts.

12. Skilled sales people always try to generate trust in themselves.

13. Successful sales people know when to talk and when to listen to their customers – and manage to achieve a balance between the two.

14. Closing the sale is your main function and is best achieved by focusing on the customer's needs. This will help you steer the customer to the "finishing line".

15. The skilled salesperson will be able to persuade the customer to buy the better item and the related accessories (that is – sell up and sell on).

2

The Trading Environment

"I try to use the environment of the business to the best of my ability; it is a showcase for our merchandise and services and I encourage customers to make the most of it. This makes it easier for me to identify the things which interest our customers and may point to their needs."

1. Introduction and Expectations

All sales people are expected to fit into the trading environment of their employer. This rather obvious point conceals a number of expectations. First of all, your firm will expect you to be successful at selling its merchandise. This could mean selling anything from the equivalent of a Rolls Royce to a cheap, battered runabout and still being comfortable about the sale.

Most retail businesses have very clear expectations about the appearance of the business and the staff who work in it. Put simply, "staff uniform" helps customers to be able to distinguish staff from visitors and also helps project an image to the shopping public. Has it occurred to you that businesses need to decide their image – and then choose the most appropriate methods of projecting it? How we dress contributes to that image to quite a large degree. This has as much relevance to the jeans and T-shirt shop as it might have in the bespoke tailors' business.

What is the purpose of this chapter? We are examining the influence of the trading environment in encouraging potential customers to enter your shop, department or restaurant in a positive frame of mind. Visitors who appreciate the ambience of the premises have already been influenced to think positively about the business, and this is an important step towards the ultimate purchase decision. The more positive the customer's frame of mind, the more likely we will close a sale – if we build on the basics.

We will consider:

- Ways in which the customer's attention may be grasped
- Customer expectations and how we may be seen
- Stock location and the importance of presentation
- Current promotions
- How the merchandise should "speak" to customers
- Observing customer behaviour

Once again, you will be able to undertake a short assignment and consider a real-life case study.

2. Grasping Customers' Attention

Most customers take as little as three seconds to pass the entrance to your business. Unless they have already made a conscious decision to visit you, the frontage and fascia, the windows and the displays all need to arrest the customer's attention and attract the customer into the premises. This is why so much investment is made into new shop fronts and why the display method used in the windows themselves is so important.

The display person's skill lies in making the merchandise look attractive. If the business looks exciting, then there is a likelihood that the customer will come in to seek more information about your products and services.

Here is our first Key Learning Point

 Sales people should always be aware of the current offer being presented to customers through the windows and promotions. They should then be able to "tune in" much more readily to one of the customer's motivations for entering the business.

So, what are these factors which attract customers to come in? Why not make a list here and check your answers against the model answer contained in Appendix 2.

List of attraction factors

1 ....

2 ....

3 ....

4 ....

5 ....

6 ....

7 ....

8 ....

9 ....

---

3. Customer Expectations

Customers who are attracted inside will expect that the pavement image created in the windows is reflected inside the business. A modern, stylish presentation will be completely ineffective if the interior is dowdy, with torn or worn carpets, tatty fixturing and miserable looking staff. Actually, the best attraction to potential customers is a busy shop or restaurant: few of us can resist that sense of curiosity created by a large number of customers inside. Conversely, a totally empty interior can be most offputting. That is why it is important for the shop to appear busy – even when it isn't. (Some managers have even been known to ask staff members to put on their coats and stand in the shop, or sit at a table, and look like customers. It is amazing how often real customers are attracted this way!).

A relaxed interior atmosphere can be created by soft music, which will help to take the cold edge off total silence. You can always tell when customers are not relaxed: they whisper to each other as if they are frightened to speak out loud for fear that they will be overheard!

What are the factors which influence customers inside the shop or department to relax and consider making a purchase? Try your hand at listing the factors which influence you – and, again, compare your answers with ours in Appendix 2.

Factors which influence customers to buy

1 ....

2 ....

3 ....

4 ....

5 ....

6 ....

7 ....

8 ....

9 ....

10 ....

11 ....

12 ....

13 ....

14 ....

15 ....

16 ....

17 ....

18 ....

19 ....

20 ....

Clearly, with such a large list of "influences", you might wonder if the sales person is really needed any more. There will always be a need for someone to:

- Find out more about the customer's needs
- Give information and advice to the customer
- Clear away customer doubts
- Persuade customers to want to buy and return to the business.

So, here is our second Key Learning Point:

The truly effective sales person is the one who knows most about the business – its layout, its stock and its systems – and can use that knowledge to exploit and endorse those influences which encourage customers to buy.

4. Stock Location

There is nothing worse than being expected to know something and to discover that you have a knowledge gap. This is a quick way to destroy confidence and every sales person needs to be confident.

So, if you have any doubts about where things are kept in your section you *must find out*. How? Don't wait to be told – *ask!* Customers will not be impressed if they have to wait while you shuffle around the place trying to find what they are looking for. If you have just transferred to a new section – or started a new job – you might find the assignment below helpful.

Assignment 1: "Treasure hunt"

At the end of this chapter you will find a space where you can draw a plan of your shop/department. (If this space is insufficient use a loose sheet of graph paper). The purpose of this "treasure hunt" is to research the locations of all the merchandise in the shop (and maybe other vital pieces of equipment, such as tape measures, order books, telephone directories, spare till rolls, etc.). When it is completed, you should have it checked by a manager or longer-serving colleague.

 Key Learning Point: The customer expects the sales person to have a detailed knowledge of the firm's products – especially where they are located and their availability. Detailed knowledge of these factors will boost your confidence and the customer's faith in you.

Experienced salespeople could use this assignment to check on the range and quantity of items which are held in the stockroom or storage areas.

5. Stock Presentation

The knowledgeable and alert sales person can make a significant difference to the:

- Quality of customer service and information provided to them
- Rotation of stock
- Identification of slow-selling lines
- Identification of low stocks (indicating the need for orders to be placed)
- Levels of sales achieved.

(Failure to rotate stock properly can also lead to stock loss through damage, wastage or even theft.)

You will have noticed that your firm has some specific ways of presenting its stock and services to customers. These have probably been decided on as a result of careful consideration of:

- How customers behave in your business
- The best ways to make the stock look attractive
- Potential for impulse purchasing
- Our own experience and expectations as customers.

Key Learning Point: Your business needs to rotate all its stock to minimise slow sellers and unsaleable lines.

6. Customer Behaviour

There are some common factors which affect the way in which shops and customer areas are designed and fitted. These points can help or hinder the selling environment.

First, in a browsing or self-selection environment people seem to prefer to circulate in a clockwise direction. (This psychological factor seems to have its origins in the fact that most of us are right-handed, thus making us more comfortable when we turn to the right.) This means that some customers may feel less comfortable if they are "influenced" to circulate in an anti-clockwise direction and may leave the sales area prematurely.

Secondly, the shop layout should take account of the basic facts about customers' physiques. Merchandise that is presented at eye level is much more likely to catch the customer's attention than items that are presented too high or too low. So, 5' 4" is an important level for fashion merchandisers and 5' 9" is a vital level for designers of fixturing in a men's shop.

Thirdly, customers like to be able to touch and feel the merchandise you are hoping to sell. The more accessible the stock item, the more likely it is that the customer will want to test it – and being able to test it is more likely to encourage the customer to buy than if the item is shut away, out of reach.

(This might create additional security risks but, generally, the increased chances of selling the products will outweigh those risks. As one designer said recently: "We must open up the stock to the risk of it being sold!").

 Key Learning Point: How has your firm tried to apply these "rules" of customer behaviour?

7. Merchandise Attraction

Some merchandise is inherently attractive. It may be its design, colour, packaging, texture or perhaps its shape or topicality and fashion appeal. There is little doubt that, if the visual appeal of the products you have to sell is enhanced, then sales will increase. These points will have led your business to present stock in particular ways – for example:

- Ties presented on, or alongside, shirts
- Jackets and skirts coordinated in displays alongside each other
- Chairs shown with tables – dressed with ornaments featured on the table
- Drinks and sweet dishes illustrated alongside main courses.

Some of the management decisions made about merchandise presentation will have a vital effect on the tasks expected of the sales person. For example, if stock is stacked onto shelves and the only way customers can see it is for sales staff to fetch it down, then staff will be spending a significant part of their day tidying up after customers and putting the stock back. (This method is used to great effect by Bennetton and their sales do not seem to be affected by this merchandising method.)

8. Customers and Impulse Purchasing

Have you noticed how many customers choose to make a purchase totally on impulse? You could hardly have said that the item they chose was an absolute necessity – in fact, you might have wondered what made them choose it in the first place. There is little doubt that once we have made up our minds to "go shopping" it is probable that we are going to make a purchase, unless we are a "definite customer". (This is the type of person who has a very specific purchase mind and will not be satisfied until it is found.)

Apart from the different ways in which merchandising units might be used to attract the customer's attention, purchases can be encouraged by auto-suggestion. For example, placing small displays of "impulse merchandise" alongside the cash or service point undoubtedly creates attention and results in increased sales (remember the sweets by the checkout in supermarkets?).

 Key Learning Point: Ticketing, graphic signs, lighted transparencies and strategically sited posters can all create additional customer impact and generate impulse sales – but only if the customer can also find the product which is illustrated.

9. Customer Awareness

As we are all customers at some time, it is important for us to remember our own likes and dislikes when we are shopping. As we have seen, many customers wish to avoid the feeling of being pressurised into making a purchase that they did not intend and therefore are somewhat defensive when it comes to their reception in the shop. It can also be said that, when we have made up our minds to investigate an item, to try it on or to seek advice which might lead to a purchase, we can become quite impatient if the staff seem not to pay us any attention. So, it is important for sales staff to remain vigilant and customer aware. This means being sensitive to those little customer signals which show that customers may be ready to make a decision (or ready for some assistance) and that we should stop what we are doing and give them our undivided attention.

 Key Learning Point: Strong sales teams – who are well led – demonstrate their customer awareness all the time.

Members of strong sales teams keep active, even though they are unable to serve customers when there are none about. They also show they are ready for action. Such sales people speak volumes about the quality of their motivation and enthusiasm – and the leadership of their managers. Discriminating customers are usually impressed by these qualities, which means they keep coming back.

Case History

When customers find it easy to buy, they do – in their thousands.

When it was first launched, the Next organisation created a "new concept" in retailing. Whole collections of fashion merchandise were brought together in branch shops throughout the country and its early success was based on making shopping and selecting the outfit as easy as possible. Instead of laying out merchandise in a conventional manner – all the blouses together, followed by all the skirts together, and all the knitwear together – the ranges were presented as a coordinated "set", mainly by colour. This made it much easier for customers to relate whole "sets" of merchandise, with the result that they purchased several items of clothing on the one visit (rather than single choices, or double choices but only after much deliberation about "which blouse goes with which skirt").

The success of this policy is now history, and the method was quickly adopted by many other fashion retailers.

---

10. Summary

The basic principles of good retailing are simple but many people make life difficult for themselves by failing to follow the most basic routines. We have seen that, if the environment is right, the sales person will find it much easier to exploit the environment and help customers relax in a happy, but professional, environment. However, little will be achieved if, after all the effort is made to provide the correct shopping environment, the customer is handled unprofessionally.

So, what does all this mean to us as customers? There is little doubt that we are impressed by a well organised sales team when we come across one. The easiest person to sell to (if you do the "right" things) is another sales person. If you perform well, there is little doubt that the knowledgeable customer will give you the order simply because you have demonstrated that you have been well trained. Contrast this reaction to the feeling you might receive when you try your hardest to attract the attention of a waiter (when he just seems – always – to be looking the other way) and you will remember how important it is to put the customer first.

11. Questionnaire

	1	2	3	4

1. A sales person is only as good as:
(a) the advertising support the firm gives them ☐ ☐ ☐ ☐
(b) the firm's pricing policy ☐ ☐ ☐ ☐
(c) their customer handling skills ☐ ☐ ☐ ☐
(d) the quality of the stock they are given to sell ☐ ☐ ☐ ☐

2. Which factor is most important to the success of the sales
   person: ☐ ☐ ☐ ☐
(a) attitude to the job and shop environment ☐ ☐ ☐ ☐
(b) attitude to people/customers ☐ ☐ ☐ ☐
(c) attitude to money and profit ☐ ☐ ☐ ☐
(d) Attitude to the firm's products. ☐ ☐ ☐ ☐

3. Sales people should ensure:
(a) they always know which of the range is being promoted
    or displayed in the window ☐ ☐ ☐ ☐
(b) they are aware of all trade promotions ☐ ☐ ☐ ☐
(c) the stock is accessible to customers at all times ☐ ☐ ☐ ☐
(d) browsing customers are not disturbed. ☐ ☐ ☐ ☐

4. The essence of the task of selling is:
(a) ensuring the firm's buyers know what customers want ☐ ☐ ☐ ☐
(b) promoting stock so it sells itself ☐ ☐ ☐ ☐
(c) making displays attractive to your customers ☐ ☐ ☐ ☐
(d) managing the shop environment. ☐ ☐ ☐ ☐

	1	2	3	4

5. When helping a customer with a purchase, it is *most* important that the sales person:
(a) can advise the customer about suitable features ☐ ☐ ☐ ☐
(b) knows where the stock is located ☐ ☐ ☐ ☐
(c) knows what is in stock (similar to customer's needs) ☐ ☐ ☐ ☐
(d) knows what is on display at present. ☐ ☐ ☐ ☐

6. Good sales service is based on:
(a) good stock situation ☐ ☐ ☐ ☐
(b) servility ☐ ☐ ☐ ☐
(c) friendliness ☐ ☐ ☐ ☐
(d) politeness. ☐ ☐ ☐ ☐

7. Sales people are only as good as:
(a) their customer handling skills ☐ ☐ ☐ ☐
(b) price competitiveness of products ☐ ☐ ☐ ☐
(c) the firm's products ☐ ☐ ☐ ☐
(d) display effectiveness. ☐ ☐ ☐ ☐

Now that you have completed these review questions, try this development question:

8. 'Sales' and special promotions outside the usual seasons should:
(a) not be resisted by staff ☐ ☐ ☐ ☐
(b) be welcomed as an aid to achieving sales targets ☐ ☐ ☐ ☐
(c) not affect normal season's trade ☐ ☐ ☐ ☐
(d) provide the opportunity to sell regular stock as well as promotion lines. ☐ ☐ ☐ ☐

Now check your answers with our model answers in Appendix 2.

Summary of Key Learning Points

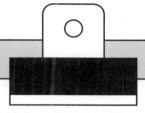

1. The sales person should always be aware of the current offer being presented to customers through the windows and current promotions.

2. The truly effective sales person is the one who knows most about the business – its layout, its stock and its systems – and can use that knowledge to exploit and endorse those influences which encourage customers to buy.

3. The customer expects the sales person to have a detailed knowledge of the firm's products – especially where they are located and their availability. Detailed knowledge of these factors will boost your confidence and the customer's faith in you.

4. Your business needs to rotate all its stock to minimise slow sellers and unsaleable lines.

5. How has your firm tried to apply these "rules" of customer behaviour?

6. Ticketing, graphic signs, lighted transparencies and strategically sited posters can all create additional customer impact and generate impulse sales – but only if the customer can also find the product which is illustrated.

7. Strong sales teams who are well led demonstrate their customer awareness, all the time.

Your shop/department plan (see Assignment 1, page 34)

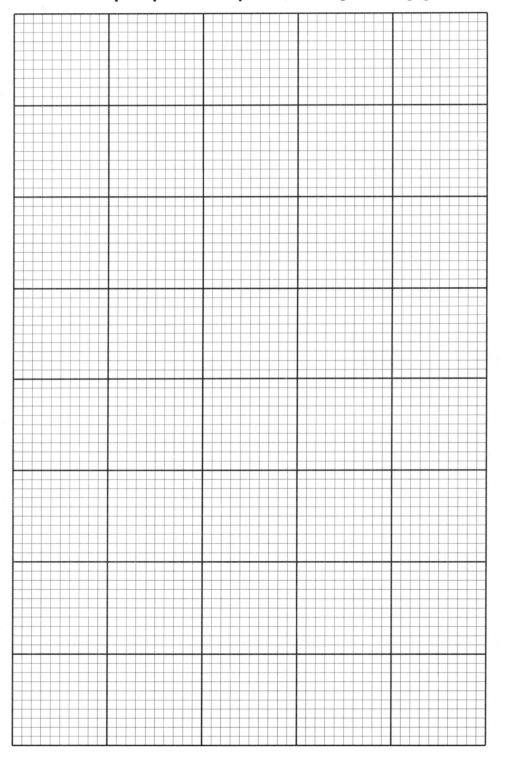

3

Who Is My Customer?

"I believe that how you greet your customer – and the reaction that creates – has a big effect on how well the customer is prepared to work with you throughout the sales interview."

1. Introduction

Experienced sales people have been heard to say that they know exactly who their customers are – just by looking at them: that is to say that they know just what kind of person the customer is and how much they can afford to spend.

Do you feel you can do this? If so, how?

There is no doubt that we *can* develop a "sixth sense" for customers – but this can also lead us down the path of many mistakes. Most people would say, today, that it is very dangerous to try to judge customers by their appearance, and even more so, by how they speak. The fact is that customers who enjoy a high disposable income may pay little importance to their appearance, and others who dress to impress may not be able to afford everything they would like.

Have you ever tried to guess the occupations of your customers? Obviously as you become more familiar with the regulars, you may get to know them better – and their own particular occupations or professions. Have you had some surprises?

This means that we have to develop a set of skills in order to assess our customers' needs, and even when we have done this we may still have some real surprises in what the customer ends up by buying.

Key Learning Point: In retailing we have to be prepared to serve every potential customer who visits the business.

Case History

Many years ago, a strange-looking character could often be seen walking around a provincial town. On hot and cold days he could be seen wearing a thick tweed coat on one shoulder but off the other and dragging the rest behind him. His unkempt appearance led many people to believe that he should be avoided.

One day this man walked into a menswear shop and the staff were very surprised when he requested a white shirt – in an extremely cultured voice! That surprise was all the greater when he asked to pay by cheque. In the days before cheque cards, a common form of identity was requested (e.g. driving licence) and the customer offered share certificates in Rolls Royce. The shop manager sanctioned the cheque, and as the customer departed he asked the assistant the correct time. Having been told the time, the customer responded by saying: "They'll be back soon!" (It transpired that the man had been an army officer and had suffered nervous trouble ever since losing a contingent of his men after sending them out on a mission, and that this accounted for his unusual appearance and behaviour.) Appearances can be very deceptive. This customer was highly educated and entirely trustworthy when it came to paying the bill.

In this chapter we are going to continue our journey in understanding more about the psychology of customers' behaviour, especially what goes through the customer's mind as he or she enters the shop. We will consider:

- Customer motivation and the mental stages the customer passes through
- Body language and the signals which may be sent
- How the sales person should "read" the signals
- How best to approach the customer.

2. Customer Motivation

As we have seen, it would be a mistake to assume that every customer is the same – thinks the same way, is interested in the same potential purchases or is even driven by the same interests and desires. Here is the second Key Learning Point:

The one truism which can be said about people is that they are all different and part of the sales person's challenge is to try to get onto their "wavelength" as quickly as possible.

Let us consider an example. Suppose that you chose to vary your outfit this morning and put on a different pair of shoes from those you have been wearing for the last few days. Perhaps they are a different colour or style that you normally keep for "best". It was raining last night and on your approach to the business from the bus-stop or station, you have to walk through an area where the road or pavement is being repaired. Unwittingly, you step in a puddle and, moments later, you realise that you must have a hole in your right shoe as that foot is feeling decidedly wet.

"Blow it!" you think (or words to that effect). "How can these shoes need repairing; I haven't worn them that much."

A closer look shows that the shoes have had harder wear than you had thought and you are now confronted with a stark choice: repair or replace. It happens that just around the corner from your business is an attractive shoe shop and so, this morning, you pause on your way past to look in the window to see if anything catches your eye.

Sure enough, your *attention* is caught by an ideal shoe style, at just the right price, tucked into the corner of the window and you make a mental note to return to the shop in your lunch break. Here is an example of the customer's *interest* being aroused – initially because the need arose for the new shoes. Actually the need to repair or replace the shoes was really *dormant* because you were unaware of it until getting your foot wet. It was quickly recognised and then it became a *motivating need* (that is to say, it drove you to take some action).

Many customer situations are like this. The customer has a desire, wish, or need to change the situation and will expect the sales person to understand (even when the precise need may remain unspoken). The pressure is on the assistant to identify the motivating needs in conversation, and this is best achieved by tactful questioning.

Another example which can sometimes lead to customer exasperation is the service in a restaurant. Our expectation for a meal may be speedy service so that it will fit into a lunch hour; or it could be that we are "filling time" in which case we might be prepared to have a slow, leisurely meal with reasonable delays between courses. If, however, the staff misread the situation (or fail to check on the customer's expectations), a great deal of embarrassment or frustration can be caused.

Key Learning Point: A simple question about the customer's needs will save considerable embarrassment – especially if you have the habit of making the wrong assumption.

3. Seeking Information

Returning to the shoe purchase example, the customer's study of the window revealed a new pair of shoes which was attractive. However, the customer now needs some crucial information about them and this can only be discovered by going inside the shop. So, the customer's next step is seeking information and here we find ourselves back at the beginning of this book – the greeting of the customer. Our customer, initially, may wish to assure him or herself that, close-to, the shoe looks as nice as it did in the window and that the advertised price seems "about right" for its style and quality.

At this point, customers may still be quite uncommitted to the purchase and want only to assure themselves that the shoes are, or are not, what they expected. It would be quite usual for this customer to be very defensive to the assistant's approach. Some customers may be thinking: "If this shoe is no good, I don't want to be talked into something else." However, should the shoe be on display in the showroom and meet the customer's expectations, the assistant is needed to satisfy the next level of information need: does the style really suit me, is it a comfortable fit, how will it wear? So, the search for the customer's correct size shoe, the process of making the customer comfortable while the shoes are fitted and tried out, are all part of the same process – the customer's search for more information. We will see in later chapters how the sales person can build on this information search to enhance the customer's *desire to own* the product by taking the buying decision.

Key Learning Point: Customers seeking information may need patient and careful handling; remember that they are probably nervous about becoming too committed too early and need space and time to arrive at their own decision.

4. Body Language

Do all these points apply to all customers? The identification of motivating needs and the search for information applies to most people. However, the customer's timing might vary a good deal. For example, the wet-footed customer might be about to embark on a shopping survey around your town, which will involve a good deal of walking, so the purchase now becomes a "disaster purchase". Provided the shoes are comfortable and are reasonably business-like, the customer will most likely buy them.

How can we tell?

As human "animals" we behave in fairly predictable ways and give off "signals" in our body language. Many visitors are not even aware that they are doing this but a skilled sales person will be able to "read" the signals sent and act accordingly to provide the right level of service.

Assignment 1

Try the following assignment and check your answers with those in Appendix 2.

What could the following signals mean and how should the sales person react?

	Signals	*Your Action*
(a)	Rushed movements	....
	Frequent glances at their watch	....
	Hurried search through stock	....
(b)	Pursed lips	....
	"Tutting" while waiting	....
	Clutching a package tightly	....
	Furrowed brow	....

---

5. What to Look for

The first signal we notice about strangers is their level of eye contact. Most people will engage us with level eye contact: that is to say, they neither look at us "down their noses" nor do they roll their eyes around or avert their gaze. People who find it difficult to look others straight in the eye tend to be thought of as a little "shifty". This signal is also reversible; your customers may be thinking the same of you, which might explain any difficulty you may have in closing sales – or perhaps you find that your customers seem to look for a second opinion about the merchandise or services you are trying to introduce. These could all be signs of a lack of trust.

 ***Key Learning Point:** It is important that you can maintain strong eye contact with your customers, or they may find it difficult to believe what you say.*

Unfortunately, body language is not quite as scientific as it might appear and it would be a mistake to assume that every customer who has a difficulty in engaging eye contact is really dishonest. The customer could have a serious eye problem – or may just be rather shy! The people who provide the greatest "threat" are those who can engage strong eye contact and still be economical (or downright misleading) about the truth.

 ***Key Learning Point:** It is the sales person who has to make the adjustments, adopting the most appropriate approach and body language to put customers at their ease.*

We will return to this point in a few moments.

Body language can be categorised into the following groups:

- Posture
- Movement
- Eye contact
- Touch
- Facial expression
- Gestures
- Appearance
- Non-verbal speech

Let us examine these points in more detail.

Posture

A great deal of information can be revealed from the ways in which people might stand, sit or walk. Our inner feelings can vary from elation and excitement to downright depression and dismay and our posture may reveal some of these feelings – perhaps as a result of past experiences. For example, a veteran soldier may still have an erect posture but the ravages of time or illness may have caused him to have a stoop. This may be a matter of great irritation to him and the assistant may detect this but it probably has nothing to do with his reactions to the assistant. Tense customers may present themselves with "wooden" smiles and body movements and convey a total dislike for the whole shopping experience. This, too, can be very disorientating, and it must be remembered that this probably has nothing to do with the current expedition (which we should try to make as pleasurable as possible).

On another dimension, customers can also appear totally at ease in all situations, even to the point of being relaxed, casual or slovenly (in dress and appearance). If you have preferences for well-dressed people, you should not let this show to such customers. Their appearance may be totally irrelevant to their spending capacity.

 Key Learning Point: Your posture will also be read by your customers. They may not be too impressed if you pose leaning against the fixtures. This might be read as a "don't care less" attitude.

Movement and space

Visitors need to be given time and space – especially those who want to browse around the merchandise. Positive customers who have a definite purchase in mind will probably show their feelings by making a direct approach to the sales person and open with a direct question or statement:

"Do you have any ...?"
"I would like to see one of those ...... in the window."

Most others are looking for information about their potential purchase and, if the assistant is too positive, the customer may think them too forward or pushy. So, it is important not to crowd the customer. Greeting politely is one thing, but rushing up close to the customer is quite another.

How near should we be? It is said that people who live in towns are used to being as close to others as a half to a full metre (regular users of buses and tubes may find themselves even closer than that!). However, those who are more used to the open spaces of the countryside may be more comfortable with greater distance between themselves and the sales person.

How can you tell which approach is acceptable?

 Key Learning Point: You should be sensitive to customers' preferences by varying your position and observing whether this has any effect on them.

Customers who back away may do so because they are losing interest in making a purchase – or it may simply be that you have encroached on their personal space and that you are now too close for comfort.

More about eye contact

We have already seen above that eye contact – or the lack of it – can be misread as untrustworthy, and that our ability to maintain strong eye contact can be most influential when dealing with customers. However, our eyes can also be most expressive. For example, surprise can be readily identified when we open our eyes wider and, if this is accompanied by a smile, the surprise can be read as a pleasant one. So, what if the customer is a trifle disappointed with the product displayed in the window now it can be seen in close-up? Eyes narrowing, or slightly closed, could be signals of disappointment and losing interest.

Customers who have thought of objections to your sales presentation may also close their eyes as you attempt to overcome a particular objection. This could be a signal of a closed mind. We also send messages to partners or friends when we hear a statement with which we disagree. A typical "eye message" would be a glance towards the heavens as we express amazement or disgust at what we have heard.

Unfortunately, many service occupations can be dangerous today. It is important that sales people are alert to the possibilities of violent behaviour, even when handling quite innocuous situations. A customer's eyes could alert you to a variety of unexpected situations – even dilated pupils, which could be a sign of drug abuse.

 Key Learning Point: If in doubt, take care of yourself!

Touch

When observing customers in your business, have you noticed that they convey a great deal of information with their hands? We sometimes say that somebody "speaks" with his or her hands, which is intended to convey that the person emphasises a great deal of their speech with hand (and sometimes even arm) movements. What does this tell us about that person? Well, at the very least it tells us that they are very expressive and cannot help giving their ideas this extra emphasis.

Please do not take this description personally. If you habitually "talk with your hands" do not become so inhibited that you cannot speak: just try to keep your enthusiasm under control.

 Key Learning Point: Observation of customers should help you "read" their minds so that you can clear away doubts about potential purchases. This should help create more sales and generate greater business opportunities.

In the main, we are taught as children that it is impolite to go around touching other people. This unwritten "rule" creates a reservation which causes us all some inhibitions in everyday life (contrast this with our neighbours in France who do not have the same reserve when it comes to physical contact and embraces). So, we tend to notice the special touching which happens to customers as they are shopping.

Touch can also be used to convey warmth and intimacy and, as such, is mostly avoided in business situations – often limited to shaking hands. However, careful touch is allowable when helping a customer to try on clothes – for example, holding out a jacket and smoothing it across the shoulders to remove any "rucks" or creases when the customer has it on.

Shopping is a very social activity and sometimes used as therapy by many lonely people. Most sales people have their "regulars" who share the latest family news and confidences with them and this can be a rewarding part of the job, provided that it does not provide too much of a distraction or is too time-consuming. Sometimes real life problems are revealed during a sales interview, and reassurance and sympathy may be sought from members of the sales team. In such situations the sales person may find sympathetic behaviour helps cement the relationship with the customer.

Case History

Moss Chemists, the retail subsidiary of Unichem and the third largest chain in the UK operating with around 400 retail chemists shops, have a sophisticated training programme for pre-registration pharmacists and pharmacy managers. This includes customer care techniques which help ensure sympathetic service in the pharmacy for customers, whose needs vary from the dispensing of vital drugs as prescribed by a doctor to the counselling of patients on potentially intricate health matters. In addition, the pharmacist is expected to lead the sales team in the shop and act as a product specialist on around 3000 ethical and non-ethical lines. Delegates on courses often describe how they are able to put uneasy minds at rest about medical conditions or a new drug with a sympathetic touch on an elderly "patient's" arm. This may be sufficient to convey an inner message: "I understand how you must feel; try not to let it get you down."

Assignment 2

Consider the following signals. How you would "read" them and what action you would take?

Signal	Possible meaning	Action
1. Finger touching lips	....	
2. Hand rubbing back of neck	....	
3. Hand brushes across forehead	....	
4. Hand rubbing nose	....	
5. Finger stretching/easing collar	....	
6. Hand holding chin	....	

Check your answers with the models in Appendix 2.

Facial expression

We are all very sensitive to facial expression and find ourselves trying to read another person's thoughts through their expressions. With some people this is easy. They are extremely "open" people and react quickly to situations with smiles, frowns, puzzlement, surprise and so on. The most sensitive part of the face in conveying expression is the eyebrows and they often reveal inner thoughts more quickly than our mouth. (Some people are ultra-cautious when it comes to conveying smiles in case the signal is misread as over-friendly).

These points are valuable when trying to convey messages, but may be highly misleading when the person has a natural facial expression which is dominated by a particular physical feature. For example:

- Naturally bushy eyebrows and a furrowed brow may project an angry expression though the customer may not be experiencing this emotion.
- A prominent chin or jaw may be read as aggressive but, again, the inner person may not have any inclination towards aggression or conflict; it might be a good idea to look for other signs (e.g. gestures) which might confirm or deny this assumption.
- A naturally smiling face may cause us to relax and not present our case so assertively and yet a smile, coupled with a sarcastic approach to the assistant, can be devastating.

Key Learning Point: After eye contact, facial expression is the most powerful method of conveying feelings to another person. Skilful sales people control their negative feelings and try always to project a positive, likeable, extrovert image to customers (even when they really feel like frowning or scowling).

Gestures

As we have seen, many people "talk" with their hands and bodies and the experienced sales person quickly learns to interpret these messages. We could categorise the common gestures as follows:

- Openness. A customer who is attempting to convince you about something he or she is saying may accompany their speech with open-handed gestures. This is really saying I have nothing to hide.
- Anger and aggression. Complaining customers may be angry and an obvious giveaway is the way in which their hands may shake or are even clenched.

- Personal discomfort. Customers may feel physical discomfort as a result of temperature changes; this is often noticeable in the winter, when the heating is turned up inside the business to benefit staff who may choose to wear rather less than they would outside. Customers with outdoor clothes on may become very hot and you may notice them constantly wiping their foreheads. This level of discomfort may discourage customers from spending time trying on clothes or spending much time in the business at all.

Appearance

Many mistakes have been made in trying to assess customers from these "signals". They probably tell us something about the customer's choice of what to wear today, on this particular outing, but not very much about the individual's taste, needs or interests in this particular visit to your shop or department. (Some very experienced retailers have identified an exception to this approach, citing the case of customers' shoes, which they believe can indicate customer taste and spending power. This could be especially valuable when you are selling clothing and fashion items.)

Non-verbal speech

Customers may use a lot of non-verbal speech and this can also convey their inner thoughts. For example, a person who sighs a lot may be expressing frustration (could they be in a hurry, or perhaps they are irritated by the sales person's presentation?). People sometimes grunt or make noises like 'Mmm'; they might also use simple words to indicate they are listening – but not much more. For example, responses like "Yes", "Right" or "I see" may not progress the sale very far but they may indicate that the customer is listening to you. Complete silence, by contrast, can be quite disconcerting and experienced sales people can feel most uncomfortable if the customer goes silent. As a result the sales person may simply babble on and on until the customer gets bored and leaves.

 Key Learning Point: Customers sometimes use the silence method to encourage the sales person to create special offers – just to close the sale. (More about this later.)

6. Summary

In this chapter we have been considering how customers "tick" and how we can "read" their thoughts. As we have seen, body language is just one way of "reading" the progress we may be making in trying to persuade a customer. It is not the only way, as we shall see in the next chapter.

Non-verbal behaviour may not of itself persuade the customer but its misuse by sales people can detract from their presentations and make them less successful.

 Key Learning Point: Try to read signals sent by customers and the "vibes" they transmit. However, you should also take great care with the signals you are sending to them.

8. Questionnaire

	1	2	3	4
1. When customers enter your business, they expect:				
(a) sales people to continue with their tasks while they browse	☐	☐	☐	☐
(b) one sales person to approach them immediately	☐	☐	☐	☐
(c) someone to ask "Can I help you?"	☐	☐	☐	☐
(d) a polite, general greeting (e.g. "Good morning").	☐	☐	☐	☐
2. The "correct" distance between sales person and customer is important because:				
(a) either party may not be all that "fresh"	☐	☐	☐	☐
(b) friendship should not be mixed with business	☐	☐	☐	☐
(c) being too close could be "offputting" to the customer	☐	☐	☐	☐
(d) being close means that you like the customer.	☐	☐	☐	☐
3. Customer's visits to your business are:				
(a) opportunities to present the widest possible service	☐	☐	☐	☐
(b) opportunities to impress them with your service	☐	☐	☐	☐
(c) opportunities to make a sale	☐	☐	☐	☐
(d) a treat.	☐	☐	☐	☐
4. Sales people should:				
(a) adopt a casual approach to their stance in the shop/ department	☐	☐	☐	☐
(b) look business-like when customers are about	☐	☐	☐	☐
(c) adopt a business-like pose all the time	☐	☐	☐	☐
(d) simply concentrate on being polite.	☐	☐	☐	☐

5. Customers who seem more "choosy" when trade is slow, should be:
(a) treated with extra encouragement ☐ ☐ ☐ ☐
(b) given more product information ☐ ☐ ☐ ☐
(c) asked to hurry up so you can spend more time with definite "prospects" ☐ ☐ ☐ ☐
(d) handled with more patience and firmness than usual. ☐ ☐ ☐ ☐

6. Some customers talk down to the sales person. Should you:
(a) approach them in exactly the same polite way as other customers – with civility and helpfulness? ☐ ☐ ☐ ☐
(b) do everything to please them and include plenty of "sirs" and "madams" in the conversation? ☐ ☐ ☐ ☐
(c) pass them over to the boss to handle? ☐ ☐ ☐ ☐
(d) complete the sale as quickly as possible? ☐ ☐ ☐ ☐

7. Are customers:
(a) individuals, who are mostly prepared to adjust to the sales person's selling techniques? ☐ ☐ ☐ ☐
(b) mostly alike and therefore responsive to a uniform customer approach? ☐ ☐ ☐ ☐
(c) individuals requiring quite separate treatment? ☐ ☐ ☐ ☐
(d) only concerned with buying at the cheapest price? ☐ ☐ ☐ ☐

8. Customers who back away from the sales person during the interview:
(a) should be followed quickly in case they are intending to leave ☐ ☐ ☐ ☐
(b) may be uncomfortable because the sales person is in their "personal space" ☐ ☐ ☐ ☐
(c) may be losing interest in the product ☐ ☐ ☐ ☐
(d) need to be closely observed for signs of security risks. ☐ ☐ ☐ ☐

Now check your answers with the model answers in Appendix 2.

Summary of Key Learning Points

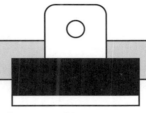

1. In retailing we have to be prepared to serve every potential customer who visits the business.

2. The one truism which can be said about people is that they are all different and part of the sales person's challenge is to try to get onto their "wavelength" as quickly as possible.

3. A simple question about the customer's needs will save considerable embarrassment – especially if you have the habit of making the wrong assumption.

4. Customers seeking information may need patient and careful handling; remember that they are probably nervous about becoming too committed too early and need space and time to arrive at their own decision.

5. So, it is important that you can maintain strong eye contact with your customers, or they may find it difficult to believe what you say.

6. It is the sales person who has to make the adjustments, adopting the most appropriate approach and body language to put customers at their ease.

7. Your posture will also be read by your customers. They may not be too impressed if you pose leaning against the fixtures. This might be read as a "don't care less" attitude.

8. You should be sensitive to customers' preferences by varying your position and observing whether this has any effect on them.

9. If in doubt, take care of yourself!

10. Observation of customers should help you "read" their minds so that you can clear away doubts about potential purchases. This should help create more sales and generate greater business opportunities.

11. After eye contact, facial expression is the most powerful method of conveying feelings to another person. Skilful sales people control their negative feelings and try always to project a positive, likeable, extrovert image to customers (even when they really feel like frowning or scowling).

12. Customers sometimes use silence to encourage the sales person to create special offers – just to close the sale.

13. Try to read signals sent by customers and the "vibes" they transmit. However, you should also take great care with the signals you are sending to them.

4

Diagnosing Customer Needs

"I must know what the customer's needs are so I can make a presentation that meets all the customer's expectations."

1. Introduction

In our previous chapters we have looked at some of the factors which affect the state of mind of customers as they consider their shopping and potential purchases, and we have discovered that our own attitudes and behaviour can make a big difference to the positive development of the sale.

The most successful sales people are those who are able to:

- Divorce their own feelings from the emotional reactions which may be generated by customers who do not behave politely towards the sales team, and
- Concentrate on helping each customer make the best and most suitable purchase.

How are some sales people so successful in achieving results, sometimes against the odds? Selling involves much more than being able to greet the customer, check the size or washing instructions with the customer, take the money, and wrap the goods. In many sections of retailing, the customer expects access to assistance from a knowledgeable person who can help with advice.

As we saw in Chapter 2, modern retailing is structured on the basis of customers doing much of the selection work for themselves. Self-selection techniques have made it possible for a whole generation of shoppers to make their own choices from a wide variety of merchandise which has been brought together by the buying team, and open stock presentation and displays have made it possible to feel and touch the stock – which can often help to develop the customer's desire to own the product.

How does this come about? Certainly not by accident. The skilled sales person has to "qualify the customer" – i.e. probing the customer's likes and dislikes, desires and preferences so that he or she can steer the customer towards a merchandise selection from the current range. This process can be quite lengthy, especially with customers who find it difficult to decide what they like or have a mental picture of their desired merchandise but find it difficult to describe it. We call this stage of selling 'Diagnosing customer needs'.

2. The Approach

When did you last visit your doctor? What happened? After the initial greeting – something like "How can I help?" – you may have given the doctor a brief description of some ailment or other. The doctor will probably have listened actively to your situation (giving you plenty of eye contact and nodding and responding with "I see" or "Yes" to show that he or she understood) and tried to discover more information to narrow down the possible causes of your discomfort.

Many customers need a similar approach. While they are interested enough to come into the business in the first instance, they are not sure what they want – and, even when they see it, they may change their minds. This does not mean that they will lose interest in buying *anything:* with your careful help and guidance they may well choose another option and a sale may still result. So, do not give up too easily!

As a customer, how many times have you had a purchase in mind and, when you have seen the product close to (or perhaps tried it on), decided that it did not suit you? Sometimes customers only have to see themselves in a mirror to see that the product is unsuitable and sometimes this realisation comes as a result of some friendly advice from the customer's partner or friend (and it might also be through the sales assistant's advice).

We return then to the central point and our first Key Learning Point:

Many customers think they know what they want, but they may actually need something different.

It is the sales person's job to help the customer establish his or her needs and then try to satisfy them. The knowledge and skills which are needed for us to carry this out include:

- Understanding of customer motivation
- Questioning skills
- Tact

- Listening skills
- How to handle customers.

3. Customer Motivation

Various approaches have been used to describe buying motives (we began to examine this topic in Chapter 3), and we are now going to cover a more sophisticated explanation. As we have seen, people are influenced by different things and, while every customer should be treated as an individual, many are motivated by similar things. We are going to look at five levels of customer motivation:

Intrinsic needs

As human beings we all share similar needs for our survival. Food and drink are obvious requirements and, at the most basic level, we could survive on bread and water. However, as we become more sophisticated – and wealthy – so our eating and buying habits change and we begin to exercise our freedom to choose a mixed diet (at its most exclusive consisting of gourmet foods). These choices are balanced against preferences for other types of expenditure which we shall re-examine in a moment.

Intrinsic needs might also include fundamental clothing, which serves the purpose of protecting us from the elements and, at this level, items may have little or no fashion value. This approach can be seen in the marketing of "basic" or "generic" products which have no benefit of a brand name and so can be sold at the bottom end of the market. There are always customers who have no interest in added value when going shopping, as well as particular groups (students, pensioners, etc.) whose restricted income makes it difficult for them to exercise customer choice. You will have noticed that some of your customers seem only to be interested in the most basic functions of products when they come shopping in your business. They are motivated by intrinsic needs.

 Key Learning Point: These customers are mostly driven by price, but often not at the expense of value. We need to demonstrate our products provide good value for money or sheer economy if price is the customer's only motivation.

Safety and security needs

Many people are unconsciously affected by a need to feel secure, i.e. to have a "roof over our heads" and a pattern of life which is reasonably predictable. These needs often come to the surface when our security is threatened in some way, perhaps through illness or unemployment, and people can react in a variety of ways. Some become stressed and go to pieces; others find themselves working even harder to achieve higher and higher goals.

Customers exhibit signs of being motivated by these needs in a variety of ways. For example, some will take few risks by choosing merchandise which they believe they can trust, perhaps through its brand reliability. A well-known brand name can attract further business simply because of its reputation and customers who make this "safe" choice are seeking to avoid the risk of disappointment of product failure later on.

Similarly, some customers will be motivated to "take a chance" on a bargain during a sale or promotion because they are being tempted to make a purchase and benefit from a short-term gain (through a price reduction, etc.). When promotions have a limited term or stock may be in short supply, customers may be persuaded to buy immediately because a risk of being overcautious may result in the merchandise being unavailable when they do decide to buy.

So, we can identify security and safety as innate motivators which can easily be identified through a sales person's probing and presentation.

 Key Learning Point: These customers are usually concerned to avoid making mistakes when purchasing. The sales person should emphasise durability, the possibility of avoiding a replacement purchase in the near future and the value of the guarantee.

Case History

Electrical retailers have discovered how powerful the security motive is by the sale of extended warranties to cover unexpected service costs on electrical goods. This has proved to be highly successful as many customers want to avoid the inconvenience and unpredictable cost of servicing the product if it should go wrong outside the guarantee period. (The success of this approach led to an enquiry by the Office of Fair Trading!)

It takes little imagination to see that while buying "peace of mind" has an important value to the customer, it will only concern the insurer if the product proves to be unreliable. Quality manufacturing processes are designed to ensure this, but the customer cannot appreciate this without some advice or guidance. Sales people need to guide customers to make the decision which brings them most comfort if they would like to see the customer become a regular.

Social needs

Many shoppers have a high level of social need. They need contact with people and use shopping as a way of increasing their opportunities for conversation. This is quite often noticeable with weekday shoppers who become regular visitors to your business – as much for the opportunity of a social chat as for the purchase of your goods or services. It would not be correct to identify such people as "lonely" just because they live their lives in a solitary way; they are really motivated by their high affiliation needs – in other words, they *need* people around them. The result is that, to them, the opportunity to chat is as important as the opportunity to make a product or service selection and this can put the assistant in a difficult position when things are busy or there are administrative tasks waiting to be undertaken.

Many regular visitors to your business will have developed an interest in it simply because of the friendly atmosphere they experience when they come in. It has been known for such people to take it as a personal insult if their regular "haunts" are changed in some way or the team is split up! In many ways, such dependence is exactly the goal of most businesses since it leads to the development of goodwill and guaranteed sales of one kind or another. The problem with this kind of dependence is that many people who are socially dependent may be more interested in the "chat" than in the business.

> **Key Learning Point: Sales people have the constant challenge of encouraging the social customer with friendly talk while also steering the topic back to the customer's needs. (This is easier said than done. The qualities required are considerable tact and lots of patience!)**

Status needs

Some people like to believe that their lifestyle marks them out as just that little different from the "rest". The use of branded goods or – more to the point – merchandise carrying a logo or brand name is generally attractive to this type of customer, whose interest in the brand name goes far beyond the expectation of a trusted or guaranteed product. Wearing a garment with an prominent logo is intended to make a statement for everyone else to see and appreciate. If the product carries an exclusive price tag, so much the better!

> **Key Learning Point: Discovering these customers' motives will often lead to a higher value sale. Failure to present the most appropriate products or services could result in no sale at all.**

Self-fulfilment

For some customers the anticipation of saving up for a particular purchase is almost as satisfying as actually owning the product. For example, most first-time house buyers are unable to afford to furnish the house fully when they move into it and have to make do with all manner of furniture and fittings probably handed down from relatives. Hire purchase, credit sales and credit cards may have made credit purchases at reasonable interest rates more accessible, but not everyone can afford the repayments (as well as the mort-gage!). So, part of the fun of home-building lies in gradually furnishing it to one's own taste.

Part of the furnishing plan might include a specifically designed leather suite, or a luxury, deep-pile carpet, or some made-to-measure curtains (say, with swags and tails), and the customer might have a great sense of achieve-ment when, at last, the product is theirs. This type of customer is usually easy to identify: they really relish the whole experience of making the purchase and sometimes have smiles like Cheshire cats especially when they have closed the purchase with you! This will have occurred to any sales person who provides a dress hire service or sells bridal gowns, and the effect can also be evident in the retail car market. However, we should not imagine that it cannot apply in many other sectors – for example, hi-fi and photographic equipment, a new set of golf clubs, new sewing or knitting machines, a new musical instrument, and perhaps a meal in the restaurant of the local luxury hotel. All these examples, and more, can become aspiration purchases.

Unfortunately, there is also an important "down-side" with such customers. If the product – or your service – goes wrong in any way or does not match up to the customer's anticipations, watch out! It may not just be a matter of being disappointed; the customer may experience a strong feeling of being let down. If the situation is not corrected quickly and reasonably generously, this type of customer can do your business untold damage by spreading word of their disappointment all round their friends – and this will of course include other potential customers in your area.

 Key Learning Point: Customers who are coming to your business for an aspiration purchase should receive excellent service (just like everyone else!). However, the sales person should try to reflect the customer's enjoyment and sense of occasion so that the whole process of the sale is remembered positively – even after the product or service has been disposed of.

Assignment 1

Make a list of *general* merchandise you have come across which would fall into the category of a status purchase . Then make a separate list of merchandise or premium services which fall into this category in *your* business.

List of status merchandise/services

General merchandise	Merchandise from your business
....	....
....	....
....	....
....	....
....	....
....	....
....	....
....	....

Many customers who are looking for status products and services are readily recognisable by the clothes they wear. Others will reveal their interests in conversation and through a little subtle questioning.

Case History

Cunard experienced difficulties with a Christmas cruise in 1994 when some of the cabins on the *Queen Elizabeth II* were not refurbished in time for the departure. The Company cancelled the holidays of some customers and offered them a full refund and a free replacement cruise for the following year. Some customers were sufficiently disappointed to threaten legal action, and others who took the cruise complained about the presence of workmen still on board completing the refurbishment. A case of an aspiration holiday purchase which went wrong.

---

4. Questioning Skills

Earlier in this chapter we saw that some customers will make an enquiry about a product or service and, when their needs are more clearly understood, it becomes apparent that the correct product to meet that need is quite different. Sometimes what the customer wants (or asks for) and what he or she actually needs may be two very different things. How should we cope with this situation?

The easiest solution would be to sell the product or service requested and let the customers discover for themselves that it is the wrong thing – by which time they may be thousands of miles away. If the customer has not been very friendly this may be an understandable reaction but it is certainly not a professional one, and is a perfect recipe for a bad reputation for the salesperson (and your business) when the customer discovers the mistake. There is no doubt that consumers have become more educated about their needs. This has come about through access to greater information from the media, consumer groups and magazines and direct from suppliers (for example, via advertising campaigns, etc.). However, mistakes are still made – sometimes with dire results.

Questioning technique assumes that the assistant is in a position to pay attention to the customer's needs and listen (and analyse) responses so that those needs are clearly understood. In professional selling circles, this process is described as "qualifying the customer" and it is a vital part of helping customers make their purchasing decisions.

Experienced sales staff see people entering the store as potential customers or "suspects" – in other words, they have come into the business to gain more information and, unless the assistant takes a hand, the decision whether to buy or not could go either way. As we have seen, some customers know exactly what they want, find it and need us only to process the sale. However, many others need help and your questioning will reveal just what kind of help or advice is needed. So, we need to find out if we can turn people who we *suspect are customers* into people who are real *"prospects"*. Prospects "qualify" for our service and we should have a good chance of making the sale a success. How?

The following techniques are most appropriate for high-value purchases because they draw information from the customer through the use of "open" questions – that is, questions which cannot easily be answered with one word such as 'Yes' or 'No'. So, the most powerful questions are those which begin with the words:

What? – Where? – Who? – When? – Why ? – How?

Case History

A recent court case involved a customer who asked about the content of a menu item as they were allergic to peanuts. They were assured that the product did not contain nuts; they ate the product and were subsequently seriously ill. Here was a case of an informed customer who was better informed than the assistant – with serious and painful consequences! (Allergy to nuts is sufficiently common that food retailers and restaurants should take food labelling really seriously.) The responsible sales person should always bear in mind that there can be a "hidden agenda" with many purchases and make doubly sure that any health and safety issues are properly discussed with the customer.

Assignment 2

Assuming you have a customer in your business who has shown some interest in a fairly expensive product, write out six questions which should deliver information that will help you decide:

(a) whether the customer will buy today and

(b) what type of product or service you should show the customer which should meet his/her needs.

1. ....

2. ....

3. ....

4. ....

5. ....

6. ....

When you have completed this assignment, compare your answers with the examples shown in Appendix 2.

Of course, no customer will be thrilled at the prospect of being faced with a barrage of questions and the real skill lies in adding your qualifying questions into the general conversation. Here is a way of doing it.

At the start, you might ask for the customer's agreement and co-operation. For example, "Do you mind if I just ask you a couple of questions?" Assuming the customer agrees, a good follow-up could be:

"What have you seen that most interests you?" or "Which do you like?", and then:

"What did you like most about it? How does it compare with the one you have at the moment?"
    Another question which should help narrow down the options even more is:

"What would you change about it, if you had the chance?"

This might deliver even more useful data if you asked about the customer's current product if he or she has one.
    Customers sometimes have a very precise timetable involved in a purchase and this can also affect what type of product you show to the customer; so why not ask:

"Did you have a particular time in mind for this purchase?"

or, if the customer is busy redecorating,

"When do you expect the room to be finished?"

If the item has to be ordered, this timing may affect what you show the customer.

6. Price

And so we come to the question of price. There are two schools of thought about establishing a customer's "price bracket" for a purchase: The *assumptive* approach and the *factual* approach.

The assumptive approach

This approach works best with smaller value purchases and for businesses whose price levels are well known in the community. The sales person does not involve the customer in any discussion of price until *after* specific products or services have been presented and described. In other words, the customer is assumed to have the money to be able to afford the products and services available in the business and, all other things being equal, can be persuaded to spend the money. In reality, customers will normally state if they are concerned or unhappy about price levels and this gives the sales person the opportunity to justify the product against the customer's expectations which were discovered earlier (see above).

The factual approach

In other circumstances (such as high-value purchases) it may be preferable to involve customers in the price discussion and a simple question will draw out their preferences. For example, you could ask:

"Would you be comfortable with a price somewhere between £x and £y?"

The advantage of this question is that it discourages the customer from focusing on the lowest price and opens up the possibility of exploring different values and qualities in the product presentation.

Finally, it should be remembered that many customers go "window shopping" and do not feel that they can spend their money without the agreement of their partner. This can be very disconcerting when you have spent considerable time with the customer and he or she then wants time to consult someone else. Many sales are lost like this as the customer goes away and may not return. The professional sales person establishes the customer's need to consult right at the beginning of the sales interview and builds in opportunities to obtain commitment to the consultation process. The conversation can then include questions designed to obtain information about the partner's likely reactions. The aim here is to avoid giving the impression that the sales person is going to take sides. The better the sales person is informed, the more likely a sale will result.

6. Listening Skills

There is little point in asking questions if we do not understand what to do with the answers. For a start, it is vital to listen to your customers – a most obvious task but one which is easier said than done. We are taught to speak at a very early age but few people are actually taught how to listen. There are four main reasons for poor listening.

Hasty conclusions

Some people make rapid judgements about the person to whom they are listening. Perhaps they have heard the beginning of the conversation before and jump to the conclusion that this customer is about to ask for exactly the same things as all those previous customers. This can be extremely annoying to the customer who prefers to be treated as an individual – even when buying precisely the same curtaining material, carpet underlay or fashion outfit as hundreds of other customers. So, why do sales people do this? The most obvious answer is that they are under time pressure to serve customers and carry out many other tasks. However, poor listening often leads to misunderstanding and irritation, neither of which is conducive to the building of goodwill.

 Key Learning Point: Be patient! Try to hear customers out before jumping to conclusions about their needs.

Dreaming

Our minds sometimes carry us off into a dreamworld, perhaps driven by an attractive thought or a preoccupying worry. This might be triggered by a conversational reference to the National Lottery and how we might spend the money if we won (!) or perhaps a sudden memory of a relative or friend who is ill and awaiting treatment. It could also be that the sales person is not motivated by the selling profession or the environment in which he or she is working and feels bored – in other words, he or she is in the wrong job. Loss of attention can also occur through other distractions: a customer passing by who you find particularly attractive, or the sound of a telephone ringing but not being answered.

The speed of the conversation process can also make a big difference to our concentration. A customer who speaks and thinks very much more slowly than you could cause you some irritation and may be the cause of your loss of attention. You may wish to prove that you are "one jump ahead" and this may not be welcomed by the customer either. When it comes to interpersonal skills, like selling, it is very difficult to conceal our inner feelings and thoughts and most customers can detect a sales person whose full attention is not being applied to them and their needs.

 Key Learning Point: Full attention and complete listening requires energy and self-discipline. Try to put some effort into listening to your customers.

Selective listening

This bad habit occurs when we turn a "deaf ear" to something the other person is trying to tell us – and then we have a convenient "loss of memory" when we have to put their request into action. For example, a waiter might have heard the request for the steak to be cooked "medium/rare" but not listened to the customer's enquiry whether a pepper sauce could be added (since this requires making a special request of the chef – and chef doesn't like special requests!).

At a different level, we are all prejudiced in some way. This can show in our reluctance to listen properly to people of a particular appearance or perhaps to those who find difficulty in expressing themselves or do so in a way which you find irritating or annoying.

 Key Learning Point: Concentrate on the ideas customers are trying to communicate and not on the methods they are using. Try not to "tune out" because the customer uses words or expressions which draw an emotional response in you.

Interrupting

Quick thinkers sometimes find themselves able to finish other people's sentences for them and are tempted to interrupt. You might have noticed this amongst your friends or colleagues and have suffered from other people's interruptions. Did you find it irritating? Most people do and therefore it is important not to interrupt or over-talk your customer.

Very talkative customers can be controlled. The skills you need are:

* Breaking eye contact
* Repeatedly breaking eye contact(!)
* Gently raising one hand a little (indicating a need to break into the conversation)
* Opening your mouth to speak – but not actually saying anything
* Seeking permission to ask a question or make a statement when the customer pauses for breath – "May I just say ...?".

 Key Learning Point: It is rude to interrupt another person while they are speaking. Try not to interrupt or over-talk them – it is impossible for either person to listen properly.

7. Active Listening

This might sound like a contradiction in terms but active listening helps both parties concentrate on what is being said. Active listeners do the following:

- Give little nods to show the point has been heard
- Maintain strong eye contact
- Use little continuity words to indicate they are still "tuned-in" – for example, "Right", "Yes", "I see".

This does not mean that the sales person can learn some simple continuity words and "tune out" of the conversation while the customer is talking. This will become very obvious to the other person and create real impatience (perhaps even the desire to leave the premises).

Key Learning Point: Active listening helps you concentrate on the customer's interests and needs while allowing you to think about how they might be met.

8. Review of Customer Handling Skills

In our first chapter we considered the personal qualities and skills which are necessary for sales people to use in developing good relationships with customers. There is no doubt that the process of diagnosing customer needs is much easier if the right customer handling skills are employed. Here is a reminder of them:

Smile!

Customers like to be helped by a cheerful, smiling person. This does not mean having a fixed, skin-deep, plastic smile – but showing a relaxed, pleasant personality. Certainly when strangers need to be relaxed and helped, the whole process is easier when the sales person is recognised by customers as a good person to do business with.

Key Learning Point: Try to project the pleasing side of your person-ality throughout the sales interview. A little charm goes a long way to impress customers.

Show interest in your customer

Maintaining eye contact and reacting to customers' needs and requests will show you have a genuine interest in them as people.

Key Learning Point: Use your facial expressions to reinforce your message – and listen actively.

Make your customer feel important

The simplest way to do this is to show them that they have your undivided attention. If there is a distraction – such as a colleague coming to you for advice or the need to answer a question from your manager – you should apologise to the customer for the interruption, explain what you are doing and that it will only take a moment. If the customer asks you a question which requires some investigation, you must tell them where you are going and why. Don't just walk off – you may know what you are doing, but they do not!

 Key Learning Point: When serving, give your customer the whole of your attention.

Use your customer's name

When you have served a customer before, it is flattering for them if you are able to remember their name and use it in conversation. This is easier if you have some record of the transaction – by the use of credit cards, cheques, etc. – and you have been able to remember it. As a customer, when you hear your name used it gives a feeling of importance and breaks down selling barriers. This contributes to an atmosphere of trust.

 Key Learning Point: Try to use customers' names whenever you can.

Be appreciative

Always say "please" and "thank you" and "goodbye" to customers, especially when they are about to leave (with or without having agreed a purchase). These finishing touches help to ensure that they return to your business when they have another need you can satisfy (and sometimes when they just need some advice!).

Key Learning Point: Your business can thrive only through satisfied customers who are pleased to return for other purchases in the future. Encourage your customers to want to come back again.

9. Questionnaire

1. Customers who are interested in the image of the products
they buy are concerned mostly with:
(a) value for money
(b) durability
(c) status attached to the product
(d) their own personal aspirations.

2. Questions are useful because:
(a) they keep the customer involved in the sales interview
(b) they stop the sales person talking
(c) they are a way of keeping customers interested
(d) they draw information which helps establish customer needs.

3. The "entry point" is:
(a) the price of the merchandise requested by the customer
(b) the price of the merchandise presented by the sales person
(c) the point of entry to your shop/department
(d) the time when the customer arrives in the business.

4. An unresponsive customer should be:
(a) encouraged to talk, by the assistant asking open questions
(b) given plenty of time to think about the products without
interference
(c) encouraged to make a selection from the goods on display
(d) asked lots of direct questions.

5. Customers who are most anxious not to make mistakes in
selecting their purchases are showing principal motivation of:
(a) prestige
(b) social needs
(c) safety and security
(d) self-fulfilment

6. When diagnosing customer needs, the sales person needs to:
(a) ask lots of questions
(b) put customers at their ease
(c) look for evidence of the customer's taste
(d) listen carefully to the customer's answers.

Now check your answers with the model answers contained in Appendix 2.

Summary of Key Learning Points

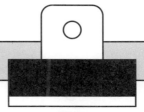

1. Many customers think they know what they want, but they may actually need something different.

2. Customers driven by price – but often not at the expense of value – are driven by "intrinsic need". The sales person needs to demonstrate that the firm's products provide good value for money or sheer economy if price is the customer's only motivation.

3. Customers driven by the need for safety and security are usually concerned to avoid making mistakes when purchasing. The sales person should emphasise durability, the possibility of avoiding a replacement purchase in the near future and the value of the guarantee.

4. Sales people have the constant challenge of encouraging the social customer with friendly talk while also steering the topic back to the customer's needs.

5. Customers driven by status needs will often make a higher value purchase. Failure to present the most appropriate products or services could result in no sale at all.

6. Customers who are coming to your business for an aspiration purchase should receive excellent service (just like everyone else!). However, the sales person should try to reflect the customer's enjoyment and sense of occasion so that the whole process of the sale is remembered positively – even after the product or service has been disposed of.

7. Full attention and complete listening requires energy and self-discipline Try to put some effort into listening to your customers.

8. Try to concentrate on the ideas customers are trying to communicate and not on the methods they are using. Try not to "tune out" because the customer uses words or expressions which draw an emotional response in you.

9. It is rude to interrupt another person while they are speaking. Try not to interrupt or over-talk them – it is impossible for either person to listen properly.

10. Active listening helps you concentrate on the customer's interests and needs while allowing you to think about how they might be met.

11. Try to project the pleasing side of your personality throughout the sales interview. A little charm goes a long way to impress customers.

12. Use your facial expressions to reinforce your message – and listen actively.

13. When serving, give your customer the whole of your attention.

14. Try to use customers' names whenever you can.

15. Business can thrive only through satisfied customers who are pleased to return for other purchases in the future. Encourage your customers to want to come back again.

5

What Is Special About the Product?

"I show customers how the product or service will meet just what they need and how the benefits will make them better off."

1. Introduction

Ultimately, the strongest buying motivator for customers must be the products and services your business supplies. Without these there would be no need for your business at all. However, it would be wrong for us to assume that every customer is driven by the same level of interest. Your firm is expected to be something of a specialist, with detailed knowledge about all the different items on your "menu", but not all customers expect to be given all the intricate details. The fact is that customers will expect to have all their questions answered but most of them will not want the detailed scientific facts.

The most common problem that customers face is sales people who have insufficient product knowledge – in fact, in some sectors, it could be described as practically non-existent. The result of this is that customers may find themselves having to make their own selections based on very little help or advice. How has this situation arisen?

The advent of self-selection and self-service brought about a need for greater information labelling so that customers could discover the more obvious facts for themselves. This works well where detailed information or advice is not needed, but when it is, the sales advisers are essential. Where do they obtain their information?

Sources of product information vary from the firm's own buying team (probably the proprietor in the smaller business) to the original manufacturer – who could be on the other side of the world. The trade press and speciality magazines also carry valuable updating information about technical aspects of products and services and these should be available for the sales team.

 Key Learning Point: Increasing your product knowledge is an essential task for every salesperson; it is a vital tool which will help you achieve success in selling.

But first we need to be clear on what product knowledge involves. Sales people generally need to know:

- What the product is
- What the product does
- How the product fulfils customers' needs and expectations
- Any other relevant information which leads to stocking, handling and selling merchandise (or services) more effectively.

Some product knowledge is required by everyone working in a business, although the depth and range of knowledge will vary according to the role of the individual. We are concerned in this chapter solely with product knowledge needed by sales people in order that customers can be properly advised when making their purchases. Where can this vital information be obtained? The simplest and most obvious source is the manager of the sales team.

However, for a whole variety of reasons, managers may not always have all the facts.

 Key Learning Point: The sales person who wishes to develop his or her own skills may need to carry out some personal research.

The following chart illustrates some sources of product information:

Source	Information type	Sources
Pamphlets	Manufacturing details; suggested uses; properties	Manufacturers; raw material suppliers
Labels	Care information; safety features; handling methods	Manufacturers; trade associations; research groups
Press	Availability; safety; range extensions; consumer data	National and trade press; consumer publications
Television	Advance information	Manufacturers; distributors
Verbal communication	Selling points	Supplier representatives
Office publications	Safety and legal requirements	HMSO; official publications
Diagrams/ models/ samples	Specifications; features use	Manufacturers; distributors
Exhibitions/trade fairs	Product history; trends	Manufacturers; distributors
Trade courses	Raw materials; construction selling points; use; after-care	BSSA training courses; open learning; books

So, this raises the question – how is the information passed on? The information chain is not always as complete as it should be. The manufacturer's technical team (designers and production staff) are responsible for choosing the technical components of the product and, in well organised businesses, will pass this data onto the sales representatives and the catalogue producers (if such a publication is produced). Sales representatives pass on this data to the buyer when the range is bought and, in turn, the buyer's information is passed onto the retail sales team when the products are taken into stock.

Obviously, it takes only one break in the information chain for vital data to be unavailable. Some larger businesses have sought to overcome this problem by producing product manuals which are passed down the line to sales staff and which can be used for staff training sessions or as reference manuals. What can be done, then, if none of these actions described form a normal part of *your* firm's practices?

This chapter identifies:

* A self-learning approach to product knowledge, and
* How this knowledge can be used to help customers' choice.

We will cover:

* A "twenty questions" approach to building up your product knowledge
* How to translate facts into the benefits which motivate customers to buy
* Powerful ways to describe your merchandise
* Deciding on the most appropriate entry point for your product presentation
* Relating benefits to customer needs
* A seven-point persuasion method to help you sweep away those product doubts.

As one sales trainer once put it: "We are going to help you make persuasive product presentations to customers who keep coming back – while the merchandise does not!"

2. Take Stock of your Knowledge

Sales people need information covering the description, use, storage and terms which will affect the selling of the merchandise. However, for maximum success, the sales person needs to be able to discriminate between the different products or services which are offered – many of which appear to meet the same fundamental purpose.

If you have heard all this before and are tempted to skip this chapter, ask yourself the following questions:

* Do you have customers regularly leaving without making a purchase?
* Are you always able to make suggestions for alternative products to those requested by customers?
* Could your level of cancellations, returns or exchanges be improved?
* Do you have a personal lack of interest in specific items or products?
* How high is your conversion rate? (i.e. how many browsers are turned into purchasers?)
* Could your average transaction value (per customer) be improved?
* How many customers are offered related sales?
* How many customers take up related items which are offered?

If you are able to identify improvements in any of these eight questions, then this section will help you.

 Key Learning Point: Sales people need to understand the three related functions:
- **typical customer needs,**
- **buying motivators, as well as**
- **the details of product knowledge.**

The three functions are totally interdependent!

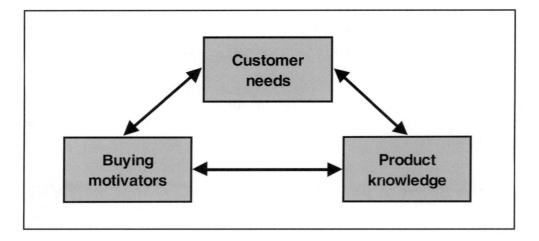

If we remove one of these three "legs", through inadequate training, the sales process may not be as effective as it should be – and the result may be lower sales achievement than could reasonably have been expected. Generally, customers are interested to know:

- Who manufactured the product
- Its trade name
- The range stocked by the firm
- Sizes and colours available
- How the product works or is operated
- Its specifications
- The meaning of any essential technical terms involved with the product
- Any safety aspects involved
- The normal price (and any specially available terms)
- Possible credit terms
- How the product should be serviced.

Information required	Sales advisers	Telephone contact staff
Supply: factors affecting	*	*
Suppliers' product ranges	*	*
Trade names	*	*
Variations available	*	
Ranges supplied by the firm	*	*
Ranges available from competitors	*	*
Comparative pricing	*	*
Product description:		
Sizes	*	*
Colours	*	*
Materials	*	*
Suitability	*	*
Customer benefits	*	*
Legal factors	*	
Technical:		
Terms	*	*
Specifications	*	*
Standards	*	*
Operating instructions	*	*
After-care	*	*
Safety and hygiene related to:		
Staff	*	
Customer	*	
Storage	*	*
Operation	*	
Administration:		
How to order	*	*
Delivery times	*	*
Sales system	*	*
Delivery system	*	
Prices:		
Recommended	*	*
Policy on discounts	*	*
Credit terms	*	*
Stock handling:		
Properties	*	*
Hazards	*	*
Packaging	*	
Promotions:		
Timing	*	*
Pricing	*	*

If we could predict exactly the questions which might be asked by customers, our preparation would be a great deal easier. As it is, the sales person needs to have acquired more data than might be needed so that the customer's commonest needs are met. To achieve this, staff who are in regular contact with customers should be expected to have a working knowledge of the following information. The chart on the previous page compares the level of information needed by sales advisers and telephone contact staff:

Most of the items listed in the table are self-evident. However, what differentiates really skilled sales people from average performers is the ability to sell from a position of strength through a knowledge of the *whole trade sector* in which they operate. In other words, they are able to emphasise the advantages of the products offered in *their business* which show better value, style or quality over those of their competitors.

Assignment 1

Using the above table, rate your knowledge of the full product range using the scale:

5 = fully knowledgeable in all aspects
4 = sound knowledge in most aspects
3 = some knowledge of some of the aspects
2 = major gaps in knowledge of this aspect
1 = little knowledge of this aspect at all

and then rate your understanding against the capabilities of one of your colleagues (possibly someone more experienced than yourself)

This "stock-take" should help you to identify gaps in existing knowledge. Once you have completed this, the next section will help with a "quiz" approach to obtaining answers to the specific issues.

3. Twenty Questions

Our second chapter helped remind us of the layout of our business and the range of products and services offered. You should also have produced a floor plan showing the general layout of your stock.

The questions in the table on page 84 will help you build up your knowledge of some specific products. We have provided an illustration of how the table might be completed:

Information required	Your score	A colleague's score
Supply: factors affecting		
Suppliers' product ranges		
Trade names		
Variations available		
Ranges supplied by the firm		
Ranges available from		
competitors		
Comparative pricing		
Product description:		
Sizes		
Colours		
Materials		
Suitability		
Customer benefits		
Legal factors		
Technical:		
Terms		
Specifications		
Standards		
Operating instructions		
After-care		
Safety and hygiene related to:		
Staff		
Customer		
Storage		
Operation		
Administration:		
How to order		
Delivery times		
Sales system		
Delivery system		
Prices:		
Recommended		
Policy on discounts		
Credit terms		
Stock handling:		
Properties		
Hazards		
Packaging		
Promotions:		
Timing		
Pricing		

Question	Answer
Description	
1. What is the product called?	Formal, long-sleeved shirt
2. What is it made of?	100% cotton
3. Who makes it?	XYZ Shirtmakers
4. What variations are there?	Collar-style, pattern, colour and fibre mix
5. What is the difference between the variations?	Fashion content, cut and ease of laundering
6. How much does it cost?	£29.95
7. How does it compare with similar items?	Mid-price/quality in the range; well known brand; good reputation for good make-up/quality. Very low rate of returns/complaints.
Use	
8. What does it do?	Covers the body with comfort and style
9. How does it do it?	Two-fold cotton woven into discreet striped fabric; twin-stitched seams and back pleats provided for comfort.
10. What are its limitations or special features?	Dual cuffs (button or links); breast pocket; full body cut; long-pointed collar.
11. How should it be worn or demonstrated?	Best worn with a coordinating colour silk tie – as shown in the display over here.
12. What are the safety aspects?	Take care in unpacking the shirt – especially with the packaging pins
13. How should it be cared for?	Follow the sewn-in washing instructions – machine or wash (60 degrees + 3*** iron)
Stock details	
14. Does it meet any relevant standards?	The supplier has the Royal Warrant and ISO 9000; it is backed by our company reputation for quality
15. What special storage requirements apply?	For pristine presentation, the shirt could be hung
16. How does the product come up to size?	It has a generous cut with full tail and standard sleeve lengths for respective collar sizes
17. Where does the product look best?	Worn with a formal business suit or smart blazer/jacket and coordinating tie
18. Who else has bought one?	Popular style amongst business people – maintains a selectivity through its range of colours and image. Brand name ensures trust amongst our regular customers.
Terms/conditions	
19. Who provides after sales care?	Normal home laundering is recommended. Please return the shirt to us if you have any problems
20. What special terms or conditions apply to its sale?	Please follow the washing instructions carefully and the garment should give excellent service.

Clearly, the researcher could add quite a lot more detail than we have illustrated here – but how far should we go? Experience shows that most customers are quite satisfied with the level of detail described in our table. However, confidence for sales people normally comes from knowledge and experience. If this is gained at a greater depth the assistant will gain that additional edge in handling demanding or discriminating customers who find it difficult to make a choice and buy from your business.

4. Customers Buy Benefits!

After all this concentration on facts, it is easy to see how product enthusiasts (or "junkies") can get carried away with a large amount of technical data, much of which has little interest for the customer. Perhaps this is the most obvious mark of an extrovert salesperson: enthusiasm for the product or service to the exclusion of the customer's concern.

Key Learning Point: "Babbling" salespeople can talk customers into a sale – and just as easily talk them out of it again!

So, how can we avoid this trap? How do we know what to say, and what not to say?

The truth is that customers are really interested only in what the product promises to do for them – in other words, how they will benefit from the purchase. Perhaps the best way of avoiding the trap is to apply the following:

Key Learning Point: Always try to present product facts to the customer by emphasising the benefits they will gain from the purchase.

Once again, this is a simple rule but one that it is easy to forget and neglect. One memory-jogger is to memorise a few "bridge or link statements" which remind us to link features with benefits. These could include:

- "This means that ..."
- "And the benefit of that is ..."
- "You will find that ..."
- "So that ..."

Every time you describe a feature of the product or service, the memory jogger will remind you to tell the customer what is in it for them.

Assignment 2

So, let us try this benefit exercise with our earlier shirt example. We have completed the first few categories and left the remainder blank for you to complete:

Feature	Link	Benefit
1. Formal, long-sleeved shirt	which means that	it is highly functional – wearable all the year round.
2. 100% cotton	and the benefit of that is	you will obtain real comfort because of its natural absorbency and insulation value.
3. XYZ Company	you can have	full confidence that the shirt will not let you down in normal use.
4. Fashionable collar, style, pattern, and colour options	and this means you have	a wide range to choose from.
5. Fibre mix varies in the range	so that you can choose	from the options of comfort, ease of laundering and price.
6.		
7.		
8.		
9.		
10.		
11.		
12.		
13.		
14.		
15.		
16.		
17.		
18.		
19.		
20.		

This might have provided you with quite a brain-teaser – but the exercise will have been really worthwhile, especially if you can now carry out the same task with your own product that you selected to work on at the end of the chapter. Why not try it out with that item now?

5. Personalising your Presentation to the Customer

Now we reach the most important part of this chapter: linking the customer's needs and interests to the benefits which can be obtained from the products you are able to offer. This is the biggest challenge faced by the sales person since it is only by qualifying the customer properly in the first place that it is possible to make this work really well. Failing to qualify the customer will leave you spraying the customer with product knowledge "buckshot" in the hope that, somehow, some of the benefits will hit an ill-defined target. When it comes to putting this into practice, it is so easy that selling should be real fun!

Supposing your shirt customer expressed an interest in a sober pattern which will go well with a formal business suit and he also wants to have a comfortable garment. We could hardly say that this customer will pay *any* price for the shirt but, if we can match the obvious needs and prove the value of the shirt (in other words ensure that the customer does not feel that the price is unjustified), we should be able to close the sale.

Key Learning Point: To be able to close sales, the sales person needs to be able to do four things:

- **Listen to and store customer needs or interests from the qualifying stage**
- **Develop an appropriate entry point for our product presentation**
- **Select and apply the most persuasive arguments which relate the product advantages to the customer's needs.**
- **Convey value through product handling.**

Listening and storing

We have already covered the listening process and there would be little point in gathering information from the customer if we were not able to store it and retrieve it while deciding what in our range might suit the customer. The process is rather like the following process diagram:

Stage	Sales person	Customer
Diagnosis	Asks open questions about needs	
		Gives factual answers
	Stores information and relates to current stock range	
		Continues to talk and browse
Presentation	Mentally selects possible product or service	
		Continues to talk and browse
	Seeks actual stock for presentation	
		Continues to talk and browse
	Verbal presentation of products or services is made	

It can be readily appreciated from this chart that a great deal of listening has to be done while the sales person is thinking about possible product or service options. This is when we use the "continuity behaviour" we described under Active Listening, i.e. those little words which acknowledge what the other person has said but actually mean very little – "Yes", "I see", "OK" or "I understand". We give the impression that we are listening while we are actually thinking about something else. This skill tends to be taken for granted until we meet a person who finds it difficult to do. Then we experience embarrassing silences as the sales person cannot think and speak. (This is sometimes so with customers as well – the ability to think and speak at the same time is not just useful to sales people.

 Key Learning Point: The duration of the listening and storing process can vary anything from a few seconds to a minute or so, but what happens during this period can have an important effect upon the progress of the sale.

Choosing an appropriate entry point to the range

This stage involves the decision of which product quality or price levels should be offered to the customer and there are several options involved:

- showing the least expensive option first

- showing the more expensive option first
- showing a middle-ranking option first.

Each of these has advantages and disadvantages.

The *least expensive* option has advantages in a price-sensitive market. If customers are looking for the cheapest option they will not be put off buying from you because of the price of the items presented. The down-side of this argument is that customers will sometimes choose to buy a more expensive item than that first requested and this option risks that some customers who might settle for that cheap option will not explore the better-quality alternatives which are on offer. This can lead to a poor average transaction value for the sales person.

Showing the *more expensive* option first has an important advantage: some customers have little idea of what they want and may be extremely impressed with the top-priced article to the extent that they will settle for that and not want to be bothered with any alternatives. This customer should be encouraged, of course.

Showing the *mid-priced option* provides a safe compromise since it is possible to add a couple of alternatives on either side of the mid-priced product – maybe an item slightly lower in price or quality closer to the entry price level, and another item at the rather better level. A simple way of remembering this option is to think of your ranges as falling into the categories:

Good	*Better*	*Best*

As can be seen, customers may choose their purchases from the three categories according to their perception of the best value and match of their needs – with a little help from the sales person, of course.

The 'good, better, best' approach also has another advantage. Because it is based on the *benefits* of each product, it is less easy for the sales person to fall into the trap of "running down" product A while building up the qualities of product B at a time when the customer may not yet have excluded Product A. Many sales people have made this mistake and lost the sale because the customer could have preferred product A until they were told about the product's disadvantages – and they were prejudiced against Product B (possibly because of the higher price which may be demanded to pay for the greater product benefits).

***Key Learning Point:** "Good, Better, Best" is a very powerful formula for product presentation because of its total flexibility and the fact that it is under the complete control of the sales person.*

Select and apply persuasive arguments in the product presentation

This is the point at which the sales person's skills with language and words can play an important part in convincing the customer. Presenting the product "sunny side up" involves emphasising the buying motivators we considered earlier – and here is another way of remembering the options:

C - R - E - W - S - A - D - E

C = Comfort
R = Reliability
E = Ego
W = Worth
S = Safety
A = Appearance
D = Durability
E = Elegance

Consider the questionnaire below. Ask yourself: "How can I use these motivators?"

Comfort:	How can I emphasise the comfort aspects of the product?
Reliability:	How can I illustrate the reliability of the product?
Ego:	Can I build in the prestige aspects of the product?
Worth:	How can I prove the worth of the product? How could I emphasise any special promotion or price value? (e.g. prices expected to rise soon)
Safety:	Is there a safety aspect to the product? How could I emphasise this?
Appearance:	How can I describe the appearance of the product in a persuasive way? (This may be a rather obvious and subjective factor but the sales person has a wonderful opportunity to describe a product's appearance in persuasive terms – e.g. colours, materials, texture, etc.)

Durability:	How can I emphasise the long-lasting quality of the materials? (and, perhaps, the enjoyment the customer will gain from owning the product?)
Elegance:	What are the style implications of the product? How does its style lift the image of the customer?

A most important element of powerful persuasion is our use of a descriptive vocabulary aimed at building up the image of the product, without risking "overselling" it. In the following illustration, we continue to use the "good, better, best" formula to enable us to "graduate" our use of adjectives as persuaders. The example is three perfumery products which can sometimes seem difficult to sell (because of the subjective nature of the scents involved and the image involved in packaging, etc.).

	Good	*Better*	*Best*
Typical price	£5 "volume"	£15 "popular"	£25 "exclusive"
Scent	"flowery"	"musky"	"alluring"
Image	"good value"	"popular"	"exclusive"
Gift value	"practical"	"attractive"	"impressive"
Economy	"haunting"	"lingering"	"long-lasting"
Packaging	"interesting"	"colourful"	"appealing"

 Key Learning Point: The most valuable tool in sales persons' "toolkits" is a persuasive and descriptive vocabulary.

It will be readily appreciated that in this market the use of the words "cheap" or "expensive" is probably best avoided since they may convey a "put down" for either the product or the customer – or both. The adjective exercise is worth pursuing with your own product range since it helps to promote differing qualities for subjective product features, even including factors such as colour and style.

Assignment 3

Using the perfumery example as a model, prepare a similar chart for a selection of products from your range. When you have completed this, check your chart with your manager. (Just one minor note of warning: take care not to get carried away and overstate qualities of products which they clearly do not have. This could lead you into misrepresentation and misapplication of trade descriptions, which is illegal.)

	Good	*Better*	*Best*
Typical price			
Scent			
Image			
Gift value			
Economy			
Packaging			

Conveying Value Through Product Handling

It may seem self-evident that the salesperson needs to show that the product is valued and this can be transmitted by the ways in which the product is handled and physically presented to the customer. For example, the forepart of the shoe is generally thought of as the most attractive part and so it is best presented first rested on one hand while the other hand holds the heel. Similarly:

- A folded jumper is best presented flat, across both hands
- An exclusive wine bottle is presented label first with one hand cradling the neck of the bottle while the other gently supports its base
- A necklace should be held gently between forefinger and thumb – rather than grasped in the full hand.

How can you apply this value approach? Ask yourself:

- How do I present my merchandise?
- Could it be improved?
- Watch more experienced sales people around you
- How do they transmit appreciation of the value of the products?
- Could you emulate their handling skills?

Key Learning Point: Value is transmitted to customers by verbal and physical presentation of the product. Show that you value the products you seek to sell by handling them as if you have saved up your own money to buy the product!

Assignment 4

As a final check on your capability of applying the ideas contained in this chapter, see if you can complete the following table with information you have discovered about an item in your own product range:

Question	Answer
Description	
1. What is the product called?	
2. What is it made of?	
3. Who makes it?	
4. What variations are there?	
5. What is the difference between the variations?	
6. How much does it cost?	
7. How does it compare with similar items?	
Use	
8. What does it do?	
9. How does it do it?	
10. What are its limitations or special features?	
11. How should it be worn or demonstrated?	
12. What are the safety aspects?	
13. How should it be cared for?	
Stock details	
14. Does it meet any relevant standards?	
15. What special storage requirements apply?	
16. How does the product come up to size?	
17. Where does the product look best?	
18. Who else has bought one?	
Terms/conditions	
19. Who provides after sales care?	
20. What special terms or conditions apply to its sale?	

Now you have completed this table, please check the details with your manager and note any information you might have missed out.

7. Summary of Key Learning Points

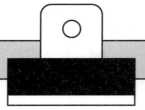

1. Increasing your product knowledge is an essential task for every sales-person; it is a vital tool which will help you achieve success in selling.

2. The sales person who wishes to develop his or her own skills may need to carry out some personal research.

3. Sales people need to understand the three related functions: typical customer needs, buying motivators and the details of product knowledge.

4. 'Babbling' salespeople can talk customers into a sale and just as easily talk them out of it again.

5. Always try to present product facts to customers by emphasising the bene-fits that they will gain from the purchase.

6. To be able to close sales, the sales person needs to be able to do four things:

* *Listen to and store customer needs or interests from the qualifying stage.*

* *Develop an appropriate entry point for our product presentation.*

* *Select and apply the most persuasive arguments which relate the product advantages to the customer's needs.*

* *Convey value through product handling.*

7. The duration of the listening and storing process can vary anything from a few seconds to a minute or so, but what happens during this period can have an important effect upon the progress of the sale.

8. 'Good, better, best' is a very powerful formula for product presentation because of its total flexibility and the fact that it is under the complete control of the sales person.

9. The most valuable tool in a sales person's 'toolkit' is a persuasive and descriptive vocabulary.

10. Value is transmitted to customers by verbal and physical presentation of the product. Show that you value the products you seek to sell by handling them as if you have saved up your own money to buy the product.

6

Involving the Customer in the Sale

"I find that many customers require quite a lot of patience – especially the better informed ones. They often ask questions and raise objections – but I prefer to have customer involvement. It is much easier to lead them towards the final decision."

1. Introduction

We have seen in earlier chapters that it is very easy for the "born sales-person" to babble away at the customer in the hope that, eventually, some of the "buckshot" will reach its target and the customer will be worn down, give in and buy the product or service. Actually this will only work in a very limited number of special cases, because most customers have very firm views of their own, and the feeble-minded customer is something of a rarity these days.

 Key Learning Point: Most customers expect to be involved in the discussion about their needs and how your offer will make them better off.

Customers' involvement will vary from wanting to touch, try on or try out the product to asking questions about it, its care or your after-sales service and even raising some objections about this item against others which they may have seen. These elements of participation are quite natural and, rather than to be seen as a nuisance, they should be encouraged as much as possible. After all, a customer who is not giving you any feedback is difficult to "read" and a customer who is not involved could be really bored – which could lead to the loss of this sale *and* of the customer.

In this chapter, we are going to consider how to control customer involvement in the sale and what to do when the customer acts in an unpredictable way and seems to go "cold" on the product or service under discussion.

First of all, let us complete a pre-session questionnaire which will alert us to the main issues involved.

2. Pre-session Questionnaire

For each of the following questions there are four alternative answers: you are asked to put the four answers in order of priority. The correct answers and the interpretations are in Appendix 2. We suggest you complete this questionnaire without looking at the Appendix, then read the chapter and complete the post-session questionnaire at the end of the chapter, and see if your "markings" have changed.

	1	2	3	4
1. The customer's involvement in the sales interview should be:				
(a) encouraged	☐	☐	☐	☐
(b) avoided	☐	☐	☐	☐
(c) viewed as a good sign	☐	☐	☐	☐
(d) considered as a theory which is unworkable in practice	☐	☐	☐	☐
2. Questions from customers during the interview should be seen as:				
(a) a bad sign – the customer will probably not buy	☐	☐	☐	☐
(b) a positive sign of involvement	☐	☐	☐	☐
(c) a good sign that the customer will buy	☐	☐	☐	☐
(d) a sign of customer involvement indicating you have the customer's attention.	☐	☐	☐	☐
3. Customers who wish to try out the product show that they are:				
(a) positively interested in the product	☐	☐	☐	☐
(b) more interested in the product than the sales person	☐	☐	☐	☐
(c) a serious prospective purchaser	☐	☐	☐	☐
(d) not interested in buying.	☐	☐	☐	☐
4. Customers who raise objections to the product in some way:				
(a) need time and space as they have received too much pressure from the sales person	☐	☐	☐	☐
(b) show that they are losing interest in the product	☐	☐	☐	☐
(c) Have not accepted all the benefits which have been presented	☐	☐	☐	☐
(d) still need to be convinced and should be "pushed a little harder".	☐	☐	☐	☐

In this chapter we shall consider:

- Customer participation – practical and questioning
- Buying signals
- Objections and how to handle them.

3. Customer Participation

It is a normal part of any sale that a customer will want to feel, touch and try out the product before buying it. This can involve a visit to the changing or fitting room or the demonstration area to see how the item looks on the customer's body or, in the case of electronics, to be able to listen to the equipment and to be able to judge the quality of the sound reproduction.

Anyone who has ever bought a bed – and regretted it later because it did not suit their needs and actually caused a bad back – will know that it would have been sensible to try out the bed in the showroom first. Similarly, the construction of a three-piece suite needs to fit the stature of the users – the depth from front to back – enabling them to sit on the seat and still rest their feet on the floor. So, trying out the chair or settee would be an important service to help the customer make the correct choice.

Demonstrating hi-fi equipment should also be carried out carefully as the potential customer might wish to listen to anything from Prince to the Royal Philharmonic Orchestra and it is possible that the reproduction needs of the different music sources may be very different. So, perhaps the equipment needs to be demonstrated with differing music sources.

 Key Learning Point: The sales person should be sensitive to the interests of the customer and some simple actions could underline the quality factors involved in the product.

For example:

- Cushions should be "plumped up" before the customer sits down
- Curtaining fabric should be gathered and draped to demonstrate how a pair of curtains might look
- Graphic equaliser settings should be used to emphasise the best response from the amplifier when replaying a CD of the last night of the Proms.

Each of these demonstrations provides an excellent opportunity for the sales person to encourage a positive comment from the customer. For example:

"Listen to that amazing bass response – that's something else, isn't it?"
"The upholstery on this settee is really sumptuous, isn't it?"
"You'll get really firm back support on this bed, won't you?"

The addition of the questions at the end of these statements are called 'mini-closes' as they encourage the customer to agree and this kind of agreement helps the overall impression that the sale is increasingly definite. (We shall return to this thought in our next chapter.)

Assignment 1

Next time you have some spare time when you are shopping, try observing your fellow shoppers – especially on the sales floor of, say, the fashion department of a nearby variety chain store. Station yourself somewhere alongside one of the major walkways and observe the number of customers who pass by the nearest display rail of blouses or skirts – and how many pause to touch and feel the fabric of the most prominent garments before continuing on their way. Many seem only to touch in order to satisfy their curiosity and one might wonder if the item is ever actually purchased. Inside your department or shop you may recognise similar trends. Perhaps we can see the touched garment as the customer's "benchmark". The item is used as a comparison with other items on display and some purchases would not occur at all if the garment was not readily available to be "tested" in this way. It is probably a small price to pay for this item to be potentially soiled and end up in the Sale when compared against all the sales which it generated!

 Key Learning Point: We all learn through our senses and, similarly, we are persuaded by various appeals to them (e.g. colour, light, texture, sound, etc.). Your customers will be more quickly persuaded when they participate in the sale.

4. Customer Reactions

Selling is all about creating customer reactions – preferably positive ones leading to a sale! However, there are occasions when responses will not be nearly so positive and this is when the special qualities of patience and determination will make all the difference to a sale or no sale.

We have seen that a customer's motivation for entering your business is probably curiosity – a demand for information about the range (or perhaps an individual item seen in the window). As the product is presented, the customer may be thinking "Is this really the product I saw in the window?" and this inner thought may even be spoken. This needs careful handling as the customer may also be thinking "I'm sure it looked *better* in the window!". So, a simple question may lead to rejection of the product if the sales person is not sensitive to what is going on in the customer's mind. How would you respond to this question? A flat "Yes" may leave the customer's inner thought still actively working towards disappointment and ultimate rejection.

Skilled sales people will find an additional feature to draw away the customer's attention:

"Yes, you can see the contrasting leathers used in this shoe – the calf leather contrasted with the luxury crocodile effect around the vamp (forepart) of the shoe. Aren't they a lovely colour?"

Or try this conversation in the furniture shop:

Customer: "Are you sure that this is the same table as shown in this advertisement? The leaves do not seem to match."
Salesperson: "Yes that's the latest homestyle range by J-plan. Our table here is in light oak which has proved a more popular version than the dark one in the brochure. You really cannot beat natural wood, with its grain variations, can you?"

How could this arise? Sometimes the image of a product is enhanced simply because it is shown under glass. This seems to enhance the "untouchable, exclusivity" of the product and, in a smaller way, cellophane or plastic wrapping can have the same effect. Inevitably, the customer's wish to see the product out of its wrapping can lead them to be disappointed with its finish and the sales person needs to compensate for this in the product presentation, perhaps by showing the product with a complementing accessory or using extra lighting to bring out the colour or "sparkle".

A typical customer may ask innumerable questions or comment in a wide variety of ways at this point:

"Do you have this in other colours?"
"Can I change it if it is wrong when I get it home?"
"Is it washable?"
"How do these wear?"
"Will this be comfortable in the sunshine?"
"How warm will this be in winter?"
"Is this quality suitable for my stairs?"
"Didn't I see this advertised at a lower price recently?"

"I'm sure that my aunt had one of these and the corner joints came apart."
"I really don't like these foreign-made products. Do they really wear well?"
"You hear a lot about poor safety with electrical goods. Are these really safe?"
"How long is the guarantee? What happens afterwards?"
"Have you sold many of these? I don't want to walk into it wherever I go!"
"This doesn't look as good as it does in the window!"

These customer reactions can be divided into a four categories:

- Questions demanding a factual response (A)
- Comments – either positive or negative (B)
- Objections (C)
- Rejections (D).

Assignment 2

Taking the list of customer comments above, categorise each one by placing the appropriate letter after each category. You will find the answers in Appendix 2.

Category

(i)   Do you have this in other colours?   ....

(ii)   Can I change it if it is wrong when I get it home?   ....

(iii)   Is it washable?   ....

(iv)   How do these wear?   ....

(v)   Will this be comfortable in the sunshine?   ....

(vi)   How warm will this be in winter?   ....

(vii)   Is this quality suitable for my stairs?   ....

(viii) Didn't I see this advertised at a lower price recently?   ....

(ix)   I'm sure that my aunt had one of these and the corner joints came apart. ....

(x)   I really don't like these foreign-made products. Do they really
        wear well?   ....

(xi)   You hear a lot about poor safety with electrical goods. Are these
        really safe?   ....

(xii)   How long is the guarantee? What happens afterwards?   ....

(xiii) Have you sold many of these? I don't want to walk into it
        wherever I go!   ....

(xiv)   This doesn't look as good as it does in the window!   ....

In terms of potential effect upon the progress of the sale, we shall now consider the above comments in order of seriousness.

5. Buying Signals

These are comments, remarks and questions which reveal that the customer is beginning to take the product seriously and becoming increasingly interested in making a purchase.

Non-verbal signals

Behaviourally, these may be noticed through the customer's body language; customers sometimes reveal their inner thoughts by something they do. For example:

- The way the customer strokes the wooden surface of a piece of cabinet furniture appreciatively
- The way the customer flexes the shoe to judge the flexibility of the leather
- The customer moving slightly towards the sales person showing warmth and interest
- The quick eye glance in response to the sales person's comment about a particular feature, perhaps accompanied by a smile.
- The way they smooth the jacket or pose with hands in skirt or trouser pockets while studying their reflection in the mirror
- That special smoothing touch of polished wood of a furniture piece which says "I really like this – I really appreciate its finish – I want it".
- The way the customer tries the item alongside something else like an accessory which says this will "go" with something I already have at home
- The sideways glance towards the partner with, perhaps, one eyebrow raised – as a way of saying: "If you like it, I'll buy it."

Verbal buying signals

Customers who have not yet given you the "green light" for the purchase need to be read carefully in case our efforts in closing the sale are mistimed or premature. So, it is important to try to read the signals which customers often send and which indicate that the customer really is thinking of making the purchase. The customer's inner thoughts and possible intentions to purchase may be revealed by comments or questions such as:

"And how much did you say this is?"
"How can I pay for this?"
"Do you accept credit cards?"
"Are you able to deliver?"
"Are you sure we could have it by Christmas?"
"Do you have my size in stock?"
"Do *you* like this?" – the question addressed to the partner for approval.

All these questions indicate that the customer really is "hot" and *will* purchase – given a little nudge.

 Key Learning Point: If buying signals are ignored or missed, the sales meeting will take longer and could even "bore" the customer and result in the loss of the sale.

With verbal involvement, however, how can you tell whether a question is a buying signal or an objection? The answer is below.

6. Customer Reactions Revisited

We shall now describe the different reactions we might expect from customers.

Questions should be dealt with honestly. Question (i) in the last assignment could be answered: "Yes, that one comes in blush pink and sky blue. We have both in stock – let me just see if we have them in your size."

 Key Learning Point: The sales person should always try to answer questions honestly.

Comments should not be ignored but dealt with positively if at all possible. The following negative customer statement might sound like a pretty conclusive hurdle with little chance of the sales person countering the statement and concluding a sale – any sale! However, a positive attitude may create a change in the customer:

Customer:"I suppose this is the new style, is it? Not very flattering, is it?" (This comment is constructed as a question but really it is an expression of a point of view and, as such, should be countered with a positive thought.)

Assistant: "I don't know, this 'off-the-shoulder' look is very fashionable and, with the casual line across the shoulder, it does allow for more movement. Will you be wanting to wear this on holiday or just as a casual jacket?" (It may be that all this year's jackets have drop shoulders and the customer dismissed the whole of the range with just one comment. So much for the concept that the customer is always right.)

We will not be looking for a disagreement, of course, just an opportunity to respond with a more positive view of the garment. You would hardly achieve much with:

"You are absolutely right, of course, but then you are describing the whole of this year's French fashion look." (The implication being that the customer may reject the whole of the range but the designers know best. This is probably not a good way of making friends with the customer!)

 Key Learning Point: Customer comments should always be dealt with positively, especially when they are negative views.

Customer Objections. Customers do not always accept the first item or idea offered to them and, if the sales person pushes too hard, the objections will increase in frequency and intensity. Objections are often a direct result of the sales person's behaviour and are not endemic to the customer.

How many objections do you tend to get from your "average" customer? If you have a lot then perhaps you are using a very positive style of selling and your customers are trying to tell you something (they may be trying to resist your pressure on them to buy the product).

Coping with objections from customers involves more than just thinking quickly and presenting "clever" responses. To do this could convey the impression that the sales person is just trying to "score points" and push the customer into the purchase for the sake of making a sale. There is a better way:

- Smile, in a friendly way – and be generally agreeable with the customer (don't snarl at, or become frustrated with, the customer)
- Show or introduce some more product benefits to the customer and then try to close the sale.

The advantage of this technique is that it gives the impression the sales person is in total control and is not thrown by the customer's objections.

Stability in the relationship should be maintained by this behaviour and the product, and its qualities, are not compromised.

 Key Learning Point: Generally, objections raised by customers tend to be genuine, and are best met with acceptance – and then turned to your advantage.

For example:

Customer: "I agree that this is the carpet I like most, but I just cannot afford the price!"
Sales person: "I agree it is not the least expensive carpet which we have in stock but then you have been looking at one of the best-quality all-wool carpets that we sell. The colour range is exclusive and the size is such that your room could be fitted out of one roll of carpet – so it would be an economical purchase."

Rejections. If the customer persists with this line of questioning, you may wonder if he or she has a real interest in buying a carpet at all. After appearing to have settled on the colour (having gone through most of the other ranges), the customer says:

" And is this quality available in those colours you showed me earlier?"
You are really in doubt about the customer's intentions, so you say: "If I can satisfy you with a good colour assortment, would you feel able to place your order and can we fit the carpet by the end of the month?"

A "No" answer shows that the customer has gone cold on the purchase (if they were ever "hot" before) and that more discussion may be quite fruitless. On the other hand, a "Yes" answer is an invitation for the sales person to close the sale on the alternative colour range and the customer will buy from that.

If the interview does not result in the customer deciding to make a purchase, the sales person must demonstrate his or her ability to lose gracefully. It is very important to "keep the door open" and encourage customers to feel that they can easily return later on. Who knows, they may not find a cheaper or better alternative anywhere else in town and may well come back to close the sale.

When it comes to sheer, blind prejudice, you should recognise when you are beaten. Comments like "I hate pink – especially this shade of puce. It really is sickly. Haven't you got anything else?" are not worthy of a response since the salesperson is most unlikely to change the customer's perception of an unacceptable colour. So, the best solution is to present an alternative colour – quickly!

Key Learning Point: *The sales person should always keep the "door open" with customers so that they will feel able to return to the business even if the current sales interview has proved unsuccessful.*

7. Summary

Let us not be totally negative in our consideration of customer involvement. The customer who would like to try on a new outfit will request a visit to the changing room and another opportunity is offered to the salesperson to support the sale. Some customers have feelings of doubt once they see the full visual effect and it is important that the sales person is available to give positive support. Quite often the customer needs a second opinion anyway.

"What do *you* think about it?" the customer may ask. "Don't you think it is a size too big? The sleeves are a little long and the skirt is too long." This may indeed be the case but it may also be true that the customer usually has this difficulty and it would be wishful thinking to expect that a stock size will fit without any alterations. The more vital question is: does the style suit the customer? Does it flatter his or her figure? If not, then it would be best to admit it and suggest the customer tries an alternative style (go back and re-qualify the customer). If, on the other hand, the garments really do have potential then you should say so, and encourage the customer to leave them with you for alteration.

These conversations are rarely quite as easy as it may sound here but careful discussion and sensitive questioning will boost the customer's confidence – without any suggestion of pushing the customer into an inappropriate decision.

Typical "soft sell" questions might include:

"Well now, how does that feel? Is it comfortable? It certainly suits you. Would you normally expect to wear formal shoes for this occasion? Would they be higher than the pair you are wearing?"

Of course these questions would not be fired in such a barrage; the discussion needs to be relaxed and sensitive and is best done in front of a full-length mirror.

Case History

Car salesmen responsible for selling BMW motor cars report that the "grin factor" evident with potential customers, who are encouraged to sit behind the wheel of their "aspirational purchase" in the showroom, is longer than with other cars. In other words, customers are so impressed with the interior – and its design – that their satisfaction shows on their faces. What better buying signal could be given?

 Key Learning Point: Through participation, customers gain the first real satisfactions of ownership. These feelings a can be so strong that they are worth exploiting as much as possible. Ask yourself: How can I enhance the "grin factor" with my merchandise?

Case History

We considered the importance of having a positive personality in an earlier chapter and this example shows how we can transmit some of that positive attitude to the customer. The importance of this is illustrated in the following story. Some years ago, two shoe sales representatives went on an export sales mission to a Third-World country. They travelled and arrived separately.

The first embarked from the airport and was horrified to see that most people in the street were barefoot. He faxed his company and said: "This mission is a waste of time. No one here seems to wear shoes so I'm coming straight home."

> The second sales person was also quick to observe that no one was wearing any footwear but he saw the situation differently. His message back to base said: "I am extending my stay here as there is an unlimited market available: no one has any shoes at present!"

8. Footnote

This chapter has covered some methods of steering the customer, and the sale, over the hurdles created by customer reactions, objections and rejections. None of this effort will be worthwhile unless we are also able to close the sale – and this is the subject of our next chapter.

10. Post Session Questionnaire

	1	2	3	4

1. The customer's involvement in the sales interview should be:
(a) encouraged
(b) avoided
(c) viewed as a good sign
(d) considered as a theory which is unworkable in practice

2. Questions from customers during the interview should be seen as:
(a) a bad sign – the customer will probably not buy
(b) a positive sign of involvement
(c) a good sign that the customer will buy
(d) a sign of customer involvement indicating you have the customer's attention.

3. Customers who wish to try out the product show that they are:
(a) positively interested in the product
(b) more interested in the product than the sales person
(c) a serious prospective purchaser
(d) not interested in buying.

4. Customers who raise objections to the product in some way:
(a) need time and space as they have received too much pressure from the sales person
(b) show that they are losing interest in the product
(c) have not accepted all the benefits which have been presented
(d) still need to be convinced and should be "pushed a little harder".

Now check your answers against the model answers in Appendix 2.

Summary of Key Learning Points

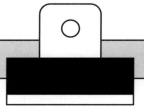

1. Most customers expect to be involved in the discussion about their needs and how your offer makes tham better off.

2. The sales person should be sensitive to the interests of the customer and some simple actions could underline the quality factors involved in the product.

3. We all learn through our senses and, similarly, we are persuaded by various appeals to them (e.g. colour, light, texture, sound, etc.). Your customers will be more quickly persuaded when they are involved in the sale.

4. If buying signals are ignored or missed, the sales meeting will take longer – and could even bore the customer and result in the loss of the sale.

5. The sales person should always try to answer questions honestly.

6. Customer comments should always be dealt with positively, especially when they are negative views.

7. Generally, objections raised by customers tend to be genuine, and are best met with acceptance and then turned to your advantage.

8. The sales person should always 'keep the door open' with customers so that they feel able to return to the business even if the current sales interview has proved to be unsuccessful.

9. Through participation, customers gain the first real satisfactions of owner-ship. These feelings can be so strong that they are worth exploiting as much as possible.

7

Close the Sale!

*"I summarise the presentation, clear away last-minute doubts, and empha-
sise the customer benefits to be gained from the purchase."*

1. Introduction

There is little point in going to all the lengths we have described in the
selling process so far unless there is a good chance that we will close the
sale. That goal is the sole purpose of all the previous steps. If we fail to bring
the customer to the "finishing tape" then all the previous effort in:

- Greeting customers and encouraging them to relax
- Qualifying the customer
- Presenting product features in benefit terms
- Encouraging customers to become involved in the sale
- Dealing with customer objections

could be wasted if the customer just says "We'll think it over" and goes away.

 **Key Learning Point: Closing the sale requires a positive attitude from
the sales person, who must have a level of determination to close
when many of the pressures seem to be against this.**

What kinds of pressure?

- Customers who might prefer to act and buy cautiously
- Changes in the way in which the retail market is working leading to
  increased price competition (how does the customer know that a similar

product is not available at a more competitive price in another shop in the vicinity of your business?)

- Greater available choice makes it difficult for some customers to decide which options to take
- Technological advances which may confuse the customer
- Lack of confidence that this is the right time to be spending the money
- A guilty conscience that the money should be spent on something or someone else.

2. Close the Sale – Now!

How can we avoid the risks presented by all these pressures? Put simply, we need to use the techniques of closing the sale and these involve:

- Ten techniques we can learn and use (each of which has different values and effects)
- An appropriate sense of timing
- An element of self-composure and self-discipline
- Supportive body language

Each of these, when used together, adds up to a powerful toolkit which will bring excellent results.

 Key Learning Point: Skilled sales people are able to close sales in a seemingly natural way and they achieve this through the best mix of technique, timing, composure and body language.

3. The Top Ten Techniques

Do closing techniques always work?

Some customers do change their minds – and others are only window shopping. How can we tell who is serious and who is not? Perhaps we should put up a sign saying: "Only serious customers will be served here."

The answer to this question lies in Chapter 4 when we considered how to "qualify the customer". So, we can now assume that we *did* qualify the customer correctly and there is no obvious reason why we should not have a real customer in front of us but, somehow, the customer is hesitating and has not yet expressed a serious commitment to buy. How can we obtain this?

The simplest answer is to use the first closing method – *ask* for the order!

Ask for it!

This is the most obvious method but also the one which is most often ignored by sales people. Why? Because they are afraid of rejection or a "No". For example:

Customer: "These are very nice trousers, I must admit."
Sales person: "Good. Would you like to buy a pair, then?"
Customer: "Just a minute, I haven't tried them on yet!"

How did you feel about this? Perhaps the salesperson brought the rejection on himself? It was rather optimistic expecting the customer to buy without trying them on – an example of good technique but poor timing.

Maybe we could give the sales person another try?

Sales person: "This seems to be the suite you prefer from all those we have looked at."
Customer: "Yes, it certainly is very comfortable. I'm just not too sure about the colour choices. The maroon colourway goes best with the curtaining material but I actually prefer the green. Which would you recommend?"
Sales Person: "I think that, if you see the colours in the daylight, you will see that either colour would be fine. Let's take the swatch to the window."
Customer: "I think you're right and green would go better with the carpet too."
Sales Person: "So, will you settle on the green, then?"
Customer: "Yes, I think so, Thank you for being so patient– it is so difficult to choose, isn't it?"

An important learning point from this last example is that the closing question grew naturally out of the conversation and seemed to be a natural resolution of the sales interview.

Key Learning Point: Closing techniques should appear to be natural developments from the sales conversation. The sales person should aim to avoid any "seams" showing; any hint that a special "formula" is being used should be avoided at all costs.

The "order form" close

This method is a natural development from the technique described above and involves just a slight variation. The main difference lies in the fact that the questions avoid any direct reference to the purchase. The closing question could therefore be:

"Would you like me to write up the order, then?"

Is this your natural language in your business? Perhaps you would prefer:

"Shall I make out the invoice or bill?"

It is important that the question sounds natural.

What would you do if the customer answers "No, thank you"? The use of a direct question runs the risk of a rejection but, if you had the feeling that the timing was right to try to close the sale, the rejection would come as rather a surprise and would raise the natural question: "Why is that?" This would be a natural reaction but the question might sound a little too pointed. It would be better to sound surprised and ask:

"I'm sorry, I have obviously misunderstood. Did you not feel that this was the best colour match/size/fitting?" (This is a cue for the customer to tell you what is wrong and why he or she may not wish to close just yet. This in itself will be a valuable piece of information as it may reveal a fundamental objection which can then be overcome.)

Key Learning Point: Gaining some reaction from the customer will enable you to judge whether you are still "on target" and should reveal any remaining barriers.

The alternative close

This method is much favoured by car salespeople – and it is based on an *assumption* that the customer *will* buy. What is not decided is which colour, style or shape is preferred. So, the question might be asked: "Which colour would you like? Red or blue?" If your timing is correct, the customer answers "red" and so commits to buying the product. A "difficult" customer might say "Who said I would buy anything?", leaving you with the need to draw out the reasons, which might seem difficult because of the way the rejection was made. But then a skilled salesperson would have noticed this fact earlier and would probably have avoided this method for fear that a rejection might be forthcoming (see also the Summary Close below).

Key Learning Point: The "Good-Better-Best" method of product presentation is most likely to lead the customer towards a final choice between two, or perhaps the three, product options which were presented. So, the either/or close is a natural follow-on to product presentation.

The summary close

This is the most natural method of closing and probably the most valuable to use with unpredictable customers. The salesperson will, in effect, summarise the sales interview so far and lead to the statement: "So, this is the one you prefer, is it?" This will be presented as if it is the natural resolution from the qualifying and presentation process (which it should be) and the net result of this should be agreement from the customer. If this is not forthcoming, the sales person should re-qualify the customer's needs.

Key Learning Point: The summary close is the most natural closing method and, properly used, the purchase decision should be made without the final question being recognised as a means of bringing the interview to a positive conclusion.

The cautionary tale

One way of motivating the customer to decide in favour of the purchase is to tell a "cautionary tale" . Typically, this might tell a story in response to a customer's question. For example:

Customer: "If I don't decide today, I suppose you have reasonable stocks and I could come back when I'm next in town, next week ?"
Sales Person: " Well, this is a busy time of the year for us and I have to say that repeat orders are very difficult to obtain. Only last week a customer failed to close a deal on another style like this and it was sold when she came back the next day. She was quite lucky: we located another one in Scotland and it will be here in three weeks' time!"
Customer: "Goodness me! I had no idea they were so scarce. I had better buy it while you have got one."

No one is suggesting that the sales person should make up stories along these lines, but letting undecided customers know what the implications might be of failing to decide to purchase today can reasonably be stated, and customers will understand the point. It is always possible that this closing strategy results in the customer saying "I'll just have to take that chance" and the sales person is left with the need to try another approach (perhaps the next one?).

Key Learning Point: Customer trust is very important so sales people should not make up stories just to motivate the customer to buy. However, it is quite acceptable to let the customer know about the possible implications of not deciding to buy today.

The "final" objection

Sometimes customers harbour a deep objection right to the end of the sale but do not want to state it – perhaps because they are afraid that it will sound trivial or even laughable to the sales person. The best solution to this could be to try to unravel this final objection – something like:

Sales Person: "I sense that you still have a reservation about this item. Could you let me know what it is and I will try to put your mind at rest?"
Customer: "Well I'm just a bit concerned about the style. You don't think it is really designed for someone younger, do you? Will everyone else be thinking that when I arrive at the cocktail party?"
Sales Person: "No, we stock this range specifically because it is suitable for all ages. It is a classic style, really, and it suits you very well. Would you like me to find someone to give you a second opinion? Perhaps that would help?"

If this seems to be acceptable, the salesperson could invite a second opinion from the manager or another experienced member of the team.

 Key Learning Point: We need to remember that some customers need the reassurance of a third party – and may then reveal a "last objection" which did not surface before. This is quite normal: it would be amazing if a sales person was able to persuade every visitor to the business, single-handed.

The conditional close

This is a helpful approach for customers who have been very slow to make up their minds and where the salesperson suspects that the latest "objection" or obstacle may just be an excuse to put the decision off still longer. The approach puts the "ball into the customer's court" when the customer raises a concern or worry by checking that this is the main or last objection. For example:

Customer: "And you are absolutely sure that we can have this Chinese rug cleaned easily?"
Sales Person: "If I can assure you completely about this, will you feel able to make the purchase today? Or do you have any other concerns?"
Customer: "No, that's all I'm worried about."
Sales Person: "Well here is the supplier's leaflet which clearly shows the cleaning instructions and we will be happy to give you an introduction to the cleaners we use, if that would help. They are very reliable."
Customer: "That sounds very helpful and reassuring. I am sure that we won't be able to do any better than this!"

At this point, the salesperson might then use the "order form close" (see above).

 Key Learning Point: The conditional close can sound a little sharp and the art is to present it in a soft way so that the customer does not feel "boxed in". It is very useful if it is felt that the customer could just be looking for excuses for not buying.

The "lost" sale approach

Many customers who are really uncertain about whether they should commit to a particular purchase feel tense and can even become somewhat withdrawn in the later stages of a sales interview. Salespeople may find this difficult to cope with as they often assume that this silent treatment is directed at them – it is dislike of them, personally, that has caused this uncertainty (and this might even be interpreted as hostility).

We must maintain a sense of balance in this situation. Salespeople cannot be liked by everyone: we are not employed to be loved – we are employed to make sales that make customers better off. So, it is inevitable that there will be occasions when we lose a sale and this is disappointing – but it will not be the end of the world. Sometimes it is possible for a customer to feel so confused or unsure that it comes as a relief just to be able to escape from the shop. The odd thing is that, once the decision is made, the customer seems to relax again and often becomes more talkative. So, this is the situation in which the conditional close might be used.

Customer: "I really am not sure about this three-piece suite; I think I am going to leave it this time."

Sales Person: "I quite understand, it is an important decision." Then, walking with customer towards the door.... "Now that you have made up your mind, I wonder if you would mind telling me what swayed your decision against this purchase today? I just sense that you still have a major doubt about it."

Customer: "Well I have nothing against you or the product as such. Frankly, I was just concerned about the durability of the fabric. You see, we have two teenagers in the house – as well as a dog and two cats – and I fear that the fabric will become stained very quickly."

Sales Person: "Oh! I see. Did I not mention the special finish which is included in the price for this product? It is an amazing stain-resistant treatment and improves the life of the fabric incredibly! Look, if I may have the opportunity to demonstrate this to you, would that help you to reconsider the purchase?"

Customer: "Yes, that would be very helpful because I just don't want to pour my money down the drain."

It is always easy to draft a "script" in a book to illustrate the point but experienced sales people who have used this approach have also found it very helpful – even though it might appear a "last ditch" attempt to win the sale. Customers do seem able to share their feelings in this way and it is possible to learn from the experience, both about your technique and your own personal style.

 Key Learning Point: Customers can be surprisingly communicative about their feelings when they have made up their minds not to buy this time. This can help the sales person identify and overcome the "last objection".

The "pros and cons" close

This is a useful technique, especially when the purchase involves several items which add together into quite a large bill. It is helpful for customers who are clearly in a quandary – should they spend all this money or not?

The whole approach during the sales interview should have emphasised the features and benefits of the products and, if the task has been fulfilled properly, the customer should have registered them well. This close suggests that the customer notes down the arguments for making the purchase and then the arguments against.

What *should* happen is that all the benefits are remembered well, but the contra arguments actually come down mainly to the cost. So, it is possible that, say, a dining-room suite has perhaps 15 benefits which can be summarised against just the one item – the cost. Sometimes, it is helpful to encourage customers to use the technique in writing, and it is then best offered at a desk or in the "closing" office or area (regularly used in car showrooms). In other situations the listing of advantages could be undertaken by the salesperson counting them up on his fingers, again leaving the impression of so many "pros" against so few "cons".

 Key Learning Point: A fluent sales person should be able to make the "pros and cons" method seem easy. The art of successful closing is to make the conversation seem entirely normal.

"I'll think it over"

How many of us must have heard this countless times? The implication is that, out of the hearing of the salesperson, the customer (possibly with a partner or friend) will talk over the purchase with less pressure; there is then perhaps a 50/50 chance that the customer will return and commit to the purchase. However, we can all think of customers about whom we would have said that they were "sure-fire certainties" but who did not return and therefore did not make the purchase.

So, the opportunity to "escape" should not be provided too easily – especially if you have the firm impression that the benefits you have to offer seem to provide a good match for the customer's needs. Once out of sight, the customer may be tempted to look at a competitor's offer and will certainly be prey to another salesperson's persuasion techniques.

Case History

One idea that an independent furnishing company uses is to provide the customers with coffee in a small informal area where they can relax and reflect on the possible purchase. The principal advantage of this is that the salesperson is nearby and can provide additional information if it is needed – and generally encourage the customer with warm feelings, occasional smiles, etc. (while appearing to undertake some small administration or housekeeping duties). This is a serious test of tact as too little contact will risk the customer deciding to go and look elsewhere and too much may defeat the object – and therefore feel "pushy".

This approach needs to be considered in conjunction with the branch/department manager as providing coffee-making facilities may not be quite as easy as it sounds (because of the fire risks). However, those firms who use this approach report that it can be successful and it does provide a comfortable solution for customers who would like to "think it over".

 Key Learning Point: Customers are more likely to be influenced to close the sale while they are in your presence. Once they have gone away, the chances of them coming back and buying are very much reduced (even when the sales person is excellent at "soft-selling").

4. Timing and Composure

It must be clear that for any of these methods to work properly, the salesperson needs to develop a good sense of timing. Too hasty action will risk the customer feeling pressurised and an approach which is too relaxed may allow the customer to develop the impression that you do not care whether a sale is made or not – and you may lose the sale.

Skilled salespeople develop a good sense of timing and expose the warm side of their personality so that customers find themselves wanting to agree with them, and this probably results in a sale. One technique is to use small closing phrases in the conversation – right from the start of the meeting. These are implied questions which seek agreement. For example:

Sales Person (presenting product): "This is the season's latest colour. It's attractive, isn't it?"
Customer: "Yes, it's just what I have been looking for."

Here, the customer might not have revealed this reaction without the sales person's statement and implied question. Other constructions which seek agreement may be used when talking generally with the customer:

"It's a nice day, isn't it?"
"We could do with some more sunshine, couldn't we?"
"The designers have come up with an excellent specification, haven't they?"
"So, you would like this delivery to arrive by Easter, wouldn't you?"
"We need to telephone you before making the delivery, don't we?"
"The benefits are clear, aren't they?"

All these little questions will gain a response from the customer and should bring acceptance or commitment just that little bit nearer and easier.

Throughout this chapter we have seen the need for the salesperson to maintain his or her composure and self-discipline. Self-control and listening skills are essential for sales "leads" to be picked up and, when closing, it is important not to rush the customer.

 Key Learning Point: When using one of the closing methods listed in this chapter, it is important to remember to pose the question and then keep quiet to let the customer respond. To keep talking invites the customer to avoid the main issue: "Would you like to buy this?" Skilled salespeople keep quiet and avoid fidgeting while the customer makes the crucial decision.

5. Body Language

This brings us to our last point in this chapter – body language. Customers are very sensitive to how you present yourself as well as what you say. An inner concern about the sale can be easily conveyed through some uncontrolled body movements. For example:

- The sales person who stands on one leg and keeps fidgeting with the other shoe may transmit a feeling of uncertainty and put the customer off
- Composure does not mean an icy expression – nor does it mean that the assistant should behave like a statue. Warm feelings still need to be transmitted, even as customers are considering a purchase which might seem quite small to the salesperson.

What should you do?

- Maintain good eye contact
- Keep still
- Have a pen ready to record the order
- Look relaxed
- Let the customer think.

 Key Learning Point: If you put the advice in this session into use, your sales will definitely increase.

- And don't forget to *smile!*

6. Questionnaire

	1	2	3	4
1. A customer who falls quiet during a sales interview:				
(a) has lost interest and the sales person should seek more reaction to the current products shown	☐	☐	☐	☐
(b) is thinking and should not be interrupted	☐	☐	☐	☐
(c) should be "closed" without delay	☐	☐	☐	☐
(d) should be offered the opportunity to think about the purchase a little more.	☐	☐	☐	☐
2. The most natural closing method is:				
(a) the either/or close	☐	☐	☐	☐
(b) the direct question close	☐	☐	☐	☐
(c) the summary close	☐	☐	☐	☐
(d) "I'll think it over".	☐	☐	☐	☐
3. If the salesperson senses that the customer is not going to buy, he or she should:				
(a) ask the customer if he or she is happy with the information given so far	☐	☐	☐	☐
(b) seek the help or support of a colleague or the manager	☐	☐	☐	☐

(c) offer a discount ☐ ☐ ☐ ☐

(d) re-summarise the features and benefits of the more
popular product or service presented. ☐ ☐ ☐ ☐

4. Where is it best to close the sale?
(a) away from the shop floor (e.g. in an office) ☐ ☐ ☐ ☐
(b) close to related merchandise ☐ ☐ ☐ ☐
(c) in the customer's home ☐ ☐ ☐ ☐
(d) out of the earshot of other customers. ☐ ☐ ☐ ☐

Now check your answers against the model answers contained in Appendix 2.

Now that you have completed these review questions, try to answer this development question:

5. At which point in a sales interview is it easiest to deal with
a second customer? While:
(a) greeting customer 1 ☐ ☐ ☐ ☐
(b) customer 1 is trying a garment on ☐ ☐ ☐ ☐
(c) closing the sale ☐ ☐ ☐ ☐
(d) the customer is considering the items shown. ☐ ☐ ☐ ☐

Summary of Key Learning Points

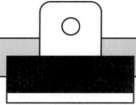

1. Closing the sale requires a positive attitude from the sales person, who must have a level of determination to close when many of the pressures seem to be against this.

2. Skilled sales people are able to close sales in a seemingly natural way and they achieve this through the best mix of technique, timing, composure and body language.

3. Closing techniques should appear to be natural developments from the sales conversation. The sales person should aim to avoid any 'seams' showing; any hint that a special formula is being used should be avoided at all costs.

4. Gaining some reaction from the customer will enable you to judge whether you are still on target and should reveal any remaining barriers.

5. The 'good-better-best' method of product presentation is most likely to lead the customer towards a final choice between two (or maybe three) product options which were presented. So, the alternative close is a natural follow-on to product presentation.

6. The summary close is the most natural closing method and, properly used, the purchase decision should be made without the final question being recognised as a means of bringing the interview to a positive conclusion.

7. Customer trust is very important, so sales people should not make up stories just to motivate the customer to buy. However, it is quite acceptable to let the customer know about the possible implications of not deciding to buy today.

8. We need to remember that some customers need the reassurance of a third party and may then reveal a 'last objection' that did not surface before. This is quite normal – it would be amazing if a sales person was able to persuade every visitor to a business, single-handed.

9. The conditional close can sound a little sharp and the art is to present it in a soft way so that the customer does not feel boxed in. It is very useful if it is felt that the customer could just be looking for an excuse for not buying.

10. Customers can be surprisingly communicative about their feelings when they have made up their minds not to buy this time. This can help the sales person identify and overcome the 'last objection'.

11. A fluent sales person should be able to make the 'pros and cons' method seem easy. The art of successful closing is to make the conversation seem entirely normal.

12. Customers are more likely to be influenced to close the sale while they are in your presence. Once they have gone away, the chances of their coming back and buying are very much reduced (even when the sales person is excellent at 'soft-selling')

13. When using one of the closing methods listed in this chapter, it is important to remember to pose the question and then keep quiet to let the customer respond. To keep talking invites the customer to avoid the main issue: 'Would you like to buy this?'

14. Skilled sales people keep quiet and avoid fidgeting while the customer makes the crucial decision.

15. If you put the advice in this chapter to use, your sales will definitely increase.

8

Will There Be Anything Else?

"When customers are in the mood to buy, I find that they will respond to suggestions about related purchases and the better quality item."

1. Introduction

Have you ever made a purchase and, when you have taken it home, begun to regret that you didn't buy the more expensive version? Most of us have economised in this way at some time and lived to regret that we did not purchase the better item with slightly more "bells and whistles" than the one we actually bought. The electronics industry is especially good at producing additional features or "gismos", each of which sets different price levels for the product and helps to discriminate one price level from another. We have also become indoctrinated by the same approach in the car market – the "XL" model has more features than the "L" and the "Ghia" is superior to the "XL". Competing products from different manufacturers are not usually labelled in this way so it falls to the sales person to be able to explain the discriminating features of one quality level against another.

For example, in the domestic electrical market, a washing machine may have a "hot and cold" fill or just a "cold fill" and this feature may endear the machine to different customers depending on their domestic water heating system. The positive sales person will quickly warm to the task of enthusing the customer with the advantages of the superior product, but not to the point of risking the loss of the customer who appreciates the better quality item but cannot afford it and so simply leaves the business a disappointed person – and probably without the purchase.

Equally, the business will earn no respect from the local community if its team has the reputation of trying to persuade visitors to spend much more than they can really afford. (Have you ever heard a customer say "You don't want to go into Blands; it will cost you an arm and a leg to get out of there."?

Key Learning Point: Professional sales people recognise that it is the customer's *interests* which need to be identified and satisfied in the sales interview, not their own.

This chapter could reasonably be subtitled "Selling up and "Selling on" as we are concentrating on the skills involved in selling the better article and also all those related accessories which enhance its value.

2. Selling Up

As we saw in our very first chapter, selling up is the process of introducing and presenting the better item in the merchandise range and encouraging the customer to consider buying it by explaining its additional benefits. This might seem obvious – in everyone's interest – but it is surprising how few sales people use this strategy. Why is this? There are several possible reasons:

- They are worried about consumer resistance to price and therefore concentrate on the cheaper options
- They do not consider the higher-priced option to be good value for money

- They would not consider buying the product themselves
- They find it easier to sell a different (perhaps less complicated) product
- They don't like it!

None of these reasons is relevant to the *customer's* position.

 Key Learning Point: The sales person does not have to like or want the product to be able to sell it. We must not stand in the way of customers buying the product, if they wish to, just because of our prejudice.

Sometimes this can work in a reverse way – the sales person withholds the better-value product (or the one with the better features) because of some curious view that the customer does not somehow deserve the product. (The psychology is rather like the petshop owner wanting strong assurances that the puppy or kitten is going to a "good home".) This might also take the form of being "difficult" with the customer because the customer has been "difficult" with the sales person. Clearly, this misguided sense of ownership of the firm's products is not in anyone's interest – but is a lot more common than many people would admit.

3. The Skills Involved

Fundamentally, selling up is a merchandise-based selling technique and will only work if the sales person has the product knowledge to be able to describe and discriminate between different product qualities. For example, the sales person who thinks that cotton sheets are much the same as poly-cotton or linen sheets may find it very difficult to sell anything better than the cheaper sheets in the range.

 Key Learning Point: Skilled sales people learn about products not in isolation, but one product in comparison with others in the range.

This knowledge may be required in some detail about the product – for example, comparison of the respective raw materials (and their advantages), comparison of manufacturing method, and even the ease with which it might be serviced or looked after. Which of these factors proves to be most persuasive will depend on the customer's buying motives and the sales person's ability in qualifying the customer (see Chapter 4).

Example

In Chapter 5 we saw that a convenient way of categorising products in customer presentations is:

Good   **Better**   **Best**

Provided that the sales person has adequate knowledge about the products, it is relatively easy to "play up" the features and qualities of one product against those of another. In the sheets example we mentioned above, the qualities could be categorised as follows:

Function	Good	Better	Best
	Poly-cotton	Cotton rich	Linen
Comfort	Soft	Absorbent	Crisp
Laundering	Warm wash	Hot wash (boil)	Hot wash
Ironing	Not essential	Iron when damp	Steam press when dry
Weight	Lightweight	Medium weight	Medium weight
Durability	Strong – subject to "pilling"	Strong, may become thin with frequent use	Exceptionally durable
Feel	Soft handle	Firm feel when laundered	Crisp, cool feel

In this example it will be readily appreciated that the sales person who has been able to classify knowledge of the product in this way has a great advantage when seeking to influence customers to appreciate the better-quality article. It could be argued in this case that, while most customers will have experienced the first two categories, the higher cost of linen sheets makes it unlikely that many customers will buy them. However, if they are in stock, customers never will consider them unless they are first introduced by the sales person.

So, apart from being able to use the knowledge of products, the other skills include:

- Confident presentation
- Encouraging the customer to participate in the sale
- Preparedness to lead the customer, and
- Coping with possible rejection.

How might the sales person develop these skills?

Confidence

Some sales people have been able to develop the role of "product consultant"; in this role they set out to act as specialist "advisers" to customers who are reliant on them for advice about the most appropriate product choices. This role is easier when the seller adopts the posture, stance, maturity and vocabulary of the experienced product specialist. This image is sometimes related to age – and mature staff members may attract far more credibility with some customers – simply because they may *look* as if they know what they are talking about!

The confident sales person speaks to customers with an air of authority. This means being able to speak on behalf of the business – using the word "we" rather than "I".

"I always recommend linen sheets. I really do not think you can beat that crisp, fresh feel when you get into bed!" is only influential and credible if the speaker can be imagined to have had in-depth experience of linen sheets. An alternative stance could be: "We find that customers who are looking for something rather better in the way of bedlinen are prepared to spend the extra on linen sheets because they know they will last much longer and will be appreciated as a luxury item. We have quite a number of regular customers who will now buy nothing else. It is surprising how tastes change, isn't it?"

Apart from the use of a little "closer" at the end of the statement, the full force of the collective experience of the whole business has been used and not just that of the sales person alone.

 Key Learning Point: Confidence increases with knowledge, practice and success.

Participation

We saw earlier in Chapter 6 that most customers like to be involved in the sale and selling up requires the sales person to be able to prove the worth of the better item. This is easier if it is possible to encourage the customer to appreciate the quality by personal experience. This could vary from:

* Opening up the cellophane for the customer to feel the fabric (of, say a shirt or duvet cover)
* Testing the controls (e.g. hi-fi)
* Touching the leather and flexing it to judge its suppleness (e.g. leather shoes)

- Having a small taste to appreciate the finer points (e.g. malt whisky)

"Don't take my word for it – try it for yourself," the sales person might say.

 Key Learning Point: Skilled sales people are not afraid to encourage the customer to participate in the sale.

Leadership

Many customers need the sales person to take the lead in the relationship. Clearly this must not be abused or used as an excuse to "rip off" the customer. However, customers can experience some strange emotions when considering a purchase. For example, a parent may be bothered by strong feelings of guilt when considering the purchase of a new suit of clothes, perhaps feeling that the money should be spent on the children instead. Sometimes this potential problem can be overcome with a light-hearted comment. For example:

- "It is good to treat yourself once in a while, isn't it?"
- "There has to be some compensation for us sometimes, doesn't there?"

Case History

The proprietor of a garage franchise for a brand of prestige cars found his own way of dealing with the "guilt syndrome". He had worked out that customers would probably not even look at the cars in the showroom unless they could afford them – and all the accessories which went with them. So, if the customer showed signs of embarrassment over the price (or resistance) he would say: "Don't worry about the price – you can afford it!" The strange thing was that he was right, and customers enjoyed being told this (and, anyway, if he was wrong, the sale could always be financed).

 Key Learning Point: Sales people should be prepared to develop their leadership ability and judge their success by the ease with which they are able to persuade customers to follow them – and make the purchase.

Rejection

Few of us like to be on the receiving end of the rejection of a piece of advice – especially when we are paid to give it. If this is carried out in a forceful way – like a snub – it can be quite upsetting. However, as we saw in Chapter 1, sales people have to be able to rise above such reverses by behaving like a little "Weeble Person". This means being able to "bounce back" by seeing rejection as a natural part of the job role – not something particular to this situation or a personal attack on you. Trying to sell the better (or extra item) will not always be successful but only by trying will it ever be successful at all.

 Key Learning Point: Experienced sales people recognise that there will be occasions when some customers' rejections "pay" for other customers' acceptances or agreements.

4. Selling On

There are four reasons for believing that related selling is in the interests of your customer:

- Enhancement of the primary purchase
- The convenience factor
- Maintenance factor
- Cost saving.

Each of these motivators can be used to lead the customer towards secondary purchases. There is no hint of manipulation or exploitation of the customer here; we are simply exploring the process of thought which most customers pass through when considering a purchase.

Enhancement

Mr Jones has an important presentation to make for his business and decides that he should invest in a new suit as his existing wardrobe is "tired". The same could also be said of his shirts, which have been put through the family washing machine many times. As a consequence, the collars do not look so good and the colours have faded a little. Mr Jones really knows that, to obtain the full effect, he will need a new suit and at least one new shirt (the tie may be in his mind as well – but not as a firm concept, yet).

After trying on the suit and being generally satisfied with its fit and style, the customer's mind turns to his presentation and any ways in which the full and persuasive effect might be dented. It is at this moment that the sales person suggests a related sale, perhaps by bringing across a complementary shirt and placing it underneath the suit jacket. It is a small distance to travel to encourage the customer to choose an appropriate tie to go with the other items and the full outfit has been chosen. All that remains is for the sale to be closed and the bill to be made out.

This scenario may seem a little far-fetched but the thought processes we have described here are accurate and often played out in reality. All things are possible once the customer's motives have been identified.

Key Learning Point: The sale is made in the mind of the customer and the buying motive may lead the customer far beyond the initial purchase.

Convenience

Customers often plan a shopping expedition – maybe into town or a main shopping centre – and your shop or department may be the planned destination:

"Where shall we go to look for a new suite?"
"Let's go and look in Johnson's. They always have something a little different there, and we could have lunch in the pub opposite."

The shopping expedition might typically involve a 15-mile drive to reach the town, and then there is the cost of car parking – and the lunch. "One-stop" shopping is exceptionally convenient, provided shoppers are able to find the purchases they are seeking. How often have you heard a customer say, "We have been looking all over town for this!" and haven't you been tempted to say "You should have come to see us first!"

It is highly likely that, if the accessories catch the imagination of the customer, the customer will buy the three-piece suite, cushions, an occasional table (or even a nest?) and maybe even a lamp to go on the table. After all, it is a great deal easier buying the full set from this store than having to walk around the rest of the town looking for something that will match the colour scheme.

Key Learning Point: The convenience factor in shopping the whole store is a very strong motivator. Customers will often be persuaded to make related purchases from the same shop or store. It beats having to walk around town looking for something that may not even exist.

Maintenance

When a customer has decided on a purchase and to spend the money, the motivation should be strong to protect and maintain the product.

Case History

Courts Furnishers operate around 200 branches throughout the UK and offer two add-on services to help customers protect their purchases. These include:

- Provision of "Scotchgard" finish for fabrics and upholstery, and
- Insurance service on the product against accidental damage and extending the warranty.

In both cases, the additional charges are relatively low in comparison with the cost of the item (e.g. a new lounge suite) and, given the cost of replacement or cleaning, the "selling-on" charge is small. Typically, the sales person may demonstrate the protection provided by "Scotchgard" through a practical demonstration. This involves spilling some coffee on two samples of fabric – one which is treated, the other not. In the case of the treated fabric, the liquid remains on the surface of the fabric and does not mark it. As can be imagined, any customers who have small children at home, or pets, would need little additional evidence to convince them to invest in the service.

The provision of insurance cover providing an extended warranty also has valuable additional benefits. Any product breakdowns after the "standard" guarantee period, which would cause potentially emotional customer complaints, would be addressed to the insurance company and not to the retailers, leaving the sales person in the customer's "good books" for recommending the insurance product.

Successful presentation of related sales depends as much upon the style and technique used as the value of the product or service itself. A positive approach is likely to be repaid by positive action by the customer. For example, a closed question might well invite rejection:

"Would you like to buy the matching belt that goes with that outfit, Madam?"
"How much is it?"
"Thirty-five pounds."
"I don't think so! Thank you".

 Key Learning Point: Any investment which helps maintain the appearance or extend the life of the product is likely to be welcomed by the customer.

Case History

A successful sales person in a shoe shop achieved high related sales through a well practised routine which led the customer towards accessories without forewarning. When bringing shoes for the customer to try on, she regularly brought out three shoe boxes. The first two boxes contained shoes, while the third was not opened or presented until after the customer had made the decision about the shoes. At this point, the assistant introduced the accessories:

"Now you have decided on the shoes, I am sure you will want to keep them looking like new. We can recommend our own shoe trees to keep the shoes in shape – and also this shoe cream which feeds the leather and keeps the shoes looking like new."

The opening of the box satisfied the customer's curiosity and concentrated the customer's attention on the related products. A further subtlety involved her posture – she maintained the kneeling position from where she had helped the customer fit the shoes. (These factors made it very difficult for the customer to refuse at least to see the products, and it seemed almost unreasonable behaviour not to buy the accessories.)

Cost saving

One of the most effective sales promotion schemes in retailing is the "multi-purchase". This means the discounting of a second item after the decision has been made to buy the first. In times of recession, customers increasingly incline to try to negotiate on price – especially when increasing the value of the purchase (for example, by choosing two pairs of shoes or a pair of shoes and a handbag). Few retailers invite discounting outside specific and legitimate promotions but the skilled sales person will not be taken by surprise if the customer seeks a discount on a multi-purchase.

Case History

A leading store group invented an appealing Christmas promotion which involved the gift of a teddy bear when the customer had spent £100. Bears have a great appeal to many customers and the "gift" attracted many, many customers across the country to make purchases up to and over the limit to enable them to benefit from this special "cost saving".

Case History

Remembering to offer related items was found to be a consistent difficulty for sales staff in one retail multiple until the firm printed a reminder on the firm's sales dockets. SSI, or Sell Second Item, as a slogan helped remind them to offer the extra item and this paid off quite often. Another business insists that the sales person records the fact that the purchase is just a "single item" on the docket – which serves the same purpose.

In an effort to encourage an increase in sales, the Swan Vesta match company ran an annual competition designed to increase sales. "Secret Shoppers" monitored the service of staff in tobacconist shops in the search for assistants who offered a box of matches (Swan Vesta's, of course) to purchasers of cigarettes or cigars.

---

5. Questionnaire

	1	2	3	4
1. Related selling involves:				
(a) making sales to friends and relations	☐	☐	☐	☐
(b) selling the more expensive item	☐	☐	☐	☐
(c) encouraging the customer to make a multi-purchase	☐	☐	☐	☐
(d) suggesting the customer buys a product related to the item already chosen.	☐	☐	☐	☐
2. When is the best time for customers to be offered related purchases?				
(a) before making the decision about the first purchase	☐	☐	☐	☐
(b) as the customer is about to pay	☐	☐	☐	☐
(c) when they have already decided to make the purchase	☐	☐	☐	☐
(d) when customers have asked for the items.	☐	☐	☐	☐
3. A strong buying motivator for related sales is:				
(a) saving money	☐	☐	☐	☐
(b) increased value	☐	☐	☐	☐
(c) the convenience factor	☐	☐	☐	☐
(d) the sales person's skill.	☐	☐	☐	☐
4. The sales person can achieve higher sales figures by:				
(a) selling the better item (better/best!)	☐	☐	☐	☐
(b) remembering to offer related items	☐	☐	☐	☐
(c) closing more sales	☐	☐	☐	☐
(d) greeting all customers.	☐	☐	☐	☐

5. An important personal quality, which makes related selling
   easier, is:
   (a) confidence
   (b) participation
   (c) "right" body language
   (d) sense of humour.

6. Sales people fail to offer related items because they are:
   (a) part-timers
   (b) thankful for a decision on the primary purchase
   (c) afraid of customer rejection
   (d) embarrassed.

Now check your answers against the model answers contained in Appendix 2.

Summary of Key Learning Points

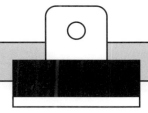

1. *Professional sales people recognise that it is the* customer's *interests which need to be identified and satisfied in the sales interview, not their own.*

2. *The sales person does not have to like or want the product to be able to sell it. We must not stand in the way of the customers buying the product if they want to – just because of our prejudice.*

3. *Skilled sales people learn abour products not in isolation, but one product in comparison with others in the range.*

4. *Confidence increases with knowledge, practice and success.*

5. *Skilled sales people are not afraid to encourage the customer to participate in the sale.*

6. *Sales people should be prepared to develop their leadership ability and judge their success by the ease with which they are able to persuade customers to follow them and make the purchase.*

7. *Experienced sales people recognise that there will be occasions when some customers' rejections 'pay' for other customers' acceptances or agreements.*

8. *The sale is made in the mind of the customer and the buying motive may lead the customer far beyond the initial purchase.*

9. *The convenience factor in shopping the whole store is a very strong motivator. Customers will often be persuaded to make related purchases from the same shop or store. It beats having to walk around town looking for something that may not even exist.*

10. *Any investment that helps maintain the appearance or extend the life of the product is likely to be welcomed by the customer.*

9

Customer Care

"Customers are the most important people in our business; we give them the best possible attention and service because, indirectly, they pay our wages."

1. Introduction

The customer care movement originated in America and was established to encourage businesses to set new standards for customer service. The techniques described in this book – when properly used – will help create sales, but it is also possible that the sales person may not always act in the best interests of the customer, or perhaps in an insincere way which could still lead to a sale but leave the customer feeling that there was something wrong about the experience. It just did not feel as if the experience was "user-friendly".

Customer care – at its most literal – means ensuring that customers receive *truly excellent service* from the moment they set foot in the business to the moment their purchases are home and in use. Most of us, at some time, have experienced just the reverse of this:

- The product which fell apart the first time we used it
- The "sales experience" where *we* did all the work and *purchased* rather than were sold to
- The "exclusive bargain" bought in a sale which turned out to be a "special purchase" that we keep meeting in our travels around town
- The almost laughable situation which occurred when we decided that we should not suppress our complaint but brought it to the attention of the supplier, only to discover that the business had no customer care policy or apparent desire to provide any satisfaction.

The customer care movement has endeavoured to change the whole culture of service to the point where customers feel "feted" and everything is done to make them feel that their business is valued by the retailer. (A good illustration of this principle in practice is DisneyWorld in California, where a theme park has been turned into a way of life – supported by hundreds of actors and actresses whose mission in life is to ensure the total enjoyment of the customer in this "fantasy land".)

Transforming an average business into a "theme park" is not the purpose of this book! However, ensuring that customers receive the best treatment and look forward to coming back surely is the responsibility of every sales person and this chapter will help identify some of the key factors involved. We are going to consider:

• Service factors involved
• Services offered by the firm
• Complaints – and how to handle them.

2. Service

For service to be viewed as a constantly improving factor in the business some specific standards need to be established so that it can be properly monitored, measured and maintained. Here are some examples of the standards which might be adopted by the customer service team in a retail business:

Customer awareness

All customers should be greeted and acknowledged wherever they are in the business – by all staff. If it appears that they might need help or attention, then this will be checked, and help offered if needed. (This might be done by the manager or anyone else on the team who happens to meet the customer. How does the customer know who has which job in your firm?)

Customers usually prefer not to have every staff member "jump" on them at every turn in the business. However, even worse, customers do not like to be ignored – and this can be the feeling if the sales person does not notice when the customer has seen something attractive and he or she needs some help. So, on balance, it is better if staff always give customers a small sign of recognition – maybe a smile – even when passing by. This gives customers who are seeking attention the opportunity to signal that they need help.

Key Learning Point: Customers expect some recognition from retail staff – regardless of who they are. A simple smile and "hello" may help to encourage customers to express their interests or needs even if you are just passing by. This may be a cue for you to find the right person to help if that is not you.

Outreach

Retailing has been compared to the entertainment business. Customers have no interest in the personal preoccupations of the retail sales team; it may be that you (or a colleague) are going through some terrible nightmare in your private life but while attending work you will be considered fit to serve customers *and* to do it with a smile. This means having the ability to bury personal problems with a view to giving full attention to the different "worlds" about you.

So, the successful "customer care assistant" is able to reach out to visitors to the firm – exposing a warm personality and smile – even though he or she may not be feeling like smiling. This also means being prepared to put yourself out for the customer even when you suspect that the customer may not end up buying the product or service (for example, the customer may want to see that last item in the range which is in the window and will mean quite a struggle to get out).

Case History

"Outreach" involves being aware of customers' needs around you. Two management trainees were carrying the day's takings to Cash Office in the department store just before closing time. They were in deep conversation about their respective plans for that evening and one of them, certainly, was totally oblivious of a customer with a pushchair approaching a flight of stairs leading to the exit. Continuing his "story", the trainee was suddenly aware that his colleague was no longer by his side but had stopped to help the customer down the stairs.

This story illustrates how easily we become preoccupied with our own conversations – about our interests, needs and plans – totally missing the needs of the customers around us. This is natural, but also wrong if we are to maintain excellent customer care standards.

Key Learning Point: Customers must come first – all the time! This sometimes means putting ourselves out when it might be inconvenient, or when we least feel up to it.

Try not to say "No"

When feeling tired or demotivated it is easy to deal with customer requests in a negative way. For example, a customer may request a brown jumper in a medium size and you know you haven't one in stock because you just looked for a previous customer. It might be tempting to tell the customer this and let him or her go and look for one somewhere else. The successful customer care assistant will express doubt:

"I don't think we have brown but I will just check. I am pretty sure we have a fashionable beige jumper in your size – but I'll have a look in the stock-room."

In the interval, while the sales person is away, the customer may have reflected on all the other shops he or she might have visited and failed to obtain the brown jumper. When the sales person returns with only the beige option, the customer might even decide to buy it and give up the idea of a brown one.

Key Learning Point: The combination of 'willingness' and 'time to reflect' will sometimes encourage customers to choose from the options you have, rather than the "impossible" choice which they were seeking.

Appeal for help!

On occasions similar to that described above sales people may get a strong feeling that the sale will be lost. It is a good idea to show the customer that you are anxious to "put yourself out" to save the sale and a good impression can be created by appealing for help from a colleague to see if there are any other alternatives to those which the customer has already seen. This can also have the advantage of providing customers with a "lead" into another sales person which can be helpful if the first sales person is having difficulty getting onto the same wavelength as the customer.

*Key Learning Point: It should not matter who makes the sale –
providing a sale is made.*

Retail is detail!

In retailing, all of us are confronted with an ever-increasing range of detail:

- Detail of stock descriptions (i.e. details of "stock-keeping units")
- Customer details (vital when taking special orders from a customer)
- Details of merchandising and display methods (which can make a huge difference to the presentation of products and therefore how the business is seen by the customer).

The catchphrase "Retail in detail" sums up one of the challenges faced by salespeople everywhere. For example, when customers wish to place a special order, the details must be recorded accurately in all respects. Otherwise the whole service is most likely to go wrong – and create positive customer dissatisfaction. Have you ever experienced:

- The product which somehow was promised to two different customers?
- The non-existent address (or telephone number) incorrectly recorded (perhaps two digits were reversed, and communication with the customer is therefore impossible?

*Key Learning Point: Customers often measure their satisfaction by
considering the number of things which go wrong in their dealings
with your business. Total customer care means that everything
should be right – first time.*

Politeness costs nothing

Customers normally respond to polite treatment – and have every right to expect it. However, social changes have meant that many people are more comfortable with less formality in business, and some may even think you are being provocative if you address them as "Sir" or "Madam". Most customers reveal, early in the conversation, something about their prefer-ences in the way you should talk to them – even if it is just the shadow of a frown across their faces – and there are times when the simple courtesies should always be used. For example, when recording a special order and asking customers for their names, it is polite for them to give their surnames first. This should be reflected back to the customer to confirm that you have heard or recorded it correctly. But it is also polite to add the expected form of address. For example:

Customer: "Would you like to order one of those then, please?"
Sales Person: "Could I just take your name and address then, please?"
Customer: "Yes, it's Jenkins"
Sales Person: "Right. Jenkins." (writes it down)

This would have been much better if the sales person had said:

"Thank you. Is that Mrs Jenkins?" (or simply had repeated "Mr Jenkins.") – a small but important contribution to the image of the sale.

Similarly, when the sales person wishes to increase his or her persuasiveness, the addition of the occasional "Sir" or "Madam" may be very effective in emphasising the customer/adviser relationship.

 Key Learning Point: Be polite at all times – and try to maintain a professional image throughout.

Keep in touch

The biggest cause of customer dissatisfaction usually lies in poor communications. Ironically, this is often most noticed when the business has tried to meet customer requirements by offering a special service like a special order.

Special orders can be a good way of building goodwill in a business; the customer feels important because the retailer has offered to take some special step on his or her behalf. What the customer may not realise is that the retailer may incur considerable extra costs in the form of handling charges (minimum order and/or postal charges) and, even then, the customer may have to wait anything from 7 to 21 days for the merchandise.

Timing of such services can be quite a problem. The customer may have a vague recollection of when the order was placed and may suddenly be aware that it seems to have taken a long time. Actually, the order was taken on a Friday in week 1 and this "feeling" occurs on the Monday of week 3. The customer is now quite sure that the order has already taken three weeks – and yet the time elapsed may have consisted of only five or six working days from the supplier's viewpoint.

"Even so," the customer might say, "Surely enough time has passed for an operative to find the product in the warehouse, book it out, pack it, and for the postal service to deliver it."

We would all probably sympathise with this viewpoint. However, the apparent delay can be made more tolerable if:

- The customer is not given an optimistic delivery date or time (it is always better to "under-promise but over-deliver")
- The sales person keeps the customer informed about any progress as it occurs. For example, an advice note should be sent to confirm receipt of the order by the supplier and this should also show whether the order is a stock item or not. This may indicate how soon the parcel might be received and could be a "trigger" for the sales person who took the order to telephone the customer to give a progress report. The cost of this action is minimal in both telephone bill and time, and yet customers are (mostly) very impressed. Strangely enough, even "bad" news of an unexpected delay will not necessarily lead to a major customer upset – provided they are kept informed.

 Key Learning Point: Successful sales people keep in touch with customers – at all times.

Assignment

If your business offers a special order service, how does it work? Do you have a special order book which contains all the details of each order? Once you have taken the order, whose task is it to place and progress the order? And who has the task of communicating with the customer? Looking back through the system, chart the progress of a typical special order and see what opportunities there were for keeping the customer "in the picture". Is there any record of this happening? Then contrast these records with those of a less efficient order when things went wrong. What lessons could be learned from this example?

When you have completed this assignment, you should discuss what you have discovered with your manager.

3. Customer Care on the Telephone

We must all have experienced intense frustration over the telephone, which can be a most infuriating (but also valuable) tool. An initial frustration can be in just trying to get connected!

Busy lines are understandable but if you have (in your view) an urgent call to make, there is little more frustrating than the constantly engaged tone. Today there are various services which can speed up customer care on the telephone. For example, the Call Waiting service encourages the talking party to end the present conversation (or at least transfer the caller) and take an incoming call.

Another frustration with the telephone is that it is a "selfish" instrument: a call will cut in on whatever task the sales person is trying to undertake; the incessant ringing "insists" on a response. How do you feel if you are visiting another business and you can hear a telephone ringing ... and ringing... and ringing? Do you feel like answering it?

If you dial into a business at 9 am and the telephone rings for more than three times without an answer, do you give up supposing that the business is closed? This is the way many people would analyse the situation. So, reasonable customer care standards would be:

- Answer the telephone in three rings (unless this is impossible through some exceptional circumstance such as a fire drill). If it is impossible to answer to this standard, the answerer should automatically give an apology for the delay
- To greet the customer with a clear statement of the name of your business (if it is an external call), a greeting (e.g. Good morning), your name, and "How may I help you?"

- When the caller asks you for some action (even if it is just to be put through to another person or department) acknowledge the request before putting it into effect
- Be prepared to take messages – and pass them on!
- Stay "friendly" even if the customer is cross, aggressive or rude
- Keep paper and pencil handy to take notes and write messages (a bound book is better than loose pieces of paper)
- Don't make people hang on if there is a delay or you need to obtain information; offer to call back
- Make call-backs a priority
- Avoid eating, drinking or other distractions while making telephone calls.

Key Learning Point: Customer care techniques must extend to telephone contact with customers. Standards should be agreed with all phone users and then monitored and assessed.

4. Services

Retailers are often obliged to offer add-on services which are essential to the achievement of the sale. These services might include:

- Delivery
- Provision of estimates or formal quotations
- Fitting and installation
- Credit
- Telephone service
- Creches

On the face of it, some of these services appear to have little to do with the core activities of selling. At first sight, the skills involved in providing a credit service may not appear to have much in common with the skills you apply in selling the product but, from the customer's viewpoint, it will be seen as an increasingly integral part of the services of your business. It may not fall to you to manage any of these activities but customers can be helped or hindered in making their purchases from your business by good quality service in these support functions.

Delivery

The firm's delivery service – whether it is subcontracted or not – should be seen as an extension of the firm's sales and marketing effort. This means that the image of the vehicles and staff needs to match the standard of the rest of the business. From the customer's viewpoint, the drivers are just an extension of the sales team and, if they fail to live up to the quality achieved in the business, this may lead to loss of goodwill (and even the loss of repeat business).

How can things go wrong? Most customers live busy lives – many are balancing work, home and family pressures all the time and a home delivery means that arrangements have to be made for someone to let the visitor in. This brings the first potential conflict: how to manage the vehicle round efficiently while also giving the customer some idea of when the delivery might be made. Also, when arriving at the customer's house or premises, delivery people should ensure that their footwear is clean before walking across carpets, etc.

> **Key Learning Point: Don't make promises you (or someone else) cannot keep. Always consult the delivery service to negotiate a special delivery "promise" before telling the customer – but also try to be helpful whenever you can.**

Failed deliveries often occur because the sales person neglected to take down some vital piece of information at the point of sale. Erroneous addresses, misspelled names, illegible handwriting and lack of location details all contribute to problems in locating the delivery point. We can help avoid these difficulties by:

- Writing clearly and legibly (BLOCK CAPITALS might be best)
- Check back details with your customer to avoid omissions
- Record any special hints on finding the location if this will help the driver (especially locations such as "3rd floor flat" which may affect how the delivery will be carried out)
- Note down the customer's telephone number in case the driver has difficulty and needs to contact the customer while on the road
- Ensuring all the necessary paperwork is linked up with the products so that the delivery is made complete (customers often complain bitterly about incomplete deliveries – hi-fi's without speakers, tables without chairs, etc.).

> **Key Learning Point: In short, try to ensure that your delivery service is helped to complete the sale by delivering the customer's purchases – first time and in full.**

Estimates and quotations

In the furnishing trades, especially, progress cannot be made to the sale without detailed measurements of the windows or floor of the room or space to be furnished. This may mean trusting the customer's own measurements or making a home visit to measure up. Here are some golden rules for estimators who have to make home visits:

- Always visit by appointment
- Ensure you have proof of identity and use it
- Be friendly but business-like – don't waste time
- Stay friendly and maintain the marketing image of the business (tidy, presentable dress, polite, etc.)
- Listen for other sales opportunities and be prepared to recommend the firm
- Check the appropriateness of the purchase the customer has in mind (for example, has the customer been informed that the carpet for the dining-room is really a bedroom quality?)
- Use a bound notebook for all the details – not loose pages – and note down factors to be taken into account (for example, times when access can be gained, doors which might need trimming, sales opportunities for new curtain track, etc.).

 Key Learning Point: Visitors to customers' homes must always remember that they are guests of the customer and ambassadors of their firms, and behave accordingly.

Installation

When the installation is to be made, those responsible must ensure that the customer continues to be impressed by the efficiency of your firm. This means:

- Being punctual
- Having all the necessary tools, equipment and materials to hand
- Bringing all necessary paperwork and records to the site
- Ensuring all waste materials are cleared from the site afterwards
- Offering to clean or sweep up loose ends before departing
- Obtaining a satisfaction note (or maybe the appropriate payment) from the customer before leaving.

Key Learning Point: Selling is often a process of encouraging the customer to buy dreams – the "remodelled dining-room", the "luxury bathroom", the "working kitchen". The installation process must ensure that the customer's dreams come true.

Credit

Today, credit is not seen by most customers or retailers as a special service. However, the efficient operation of a credit system is important: it can make or mar the vital part of the sale when the customer may have second thoughts. Credit could be taken to include:

- Credit card transactions
- Hire purchase agreements
- House credit transactions (own accounts)

Each of these transactions bring its own risks and opportunities and we shall consider technical aspects of such transactions in the next chapter. For the moment it should be remembered that customers may be asked to reveal details of their private lives before the paperwork can be completed and that they may prefer for this to be done in a relatively private area. In some businesses a "closing" office or room may be used to help establish the right atmosphere; in others the customer is encouraged to choose the most comfortable place. For example, the sales person might ask the customer to choose: "Are you comfortable completing the paperwork here or would you prefer to come to the office?" Balancing clipboards and documents on the knee may not be everyone's preference – but, equally, some customers may be intimidated by the thought of "going into the office".

Key Learning Point: Customers may prefer to choose the location for the completion of the credit paperwork. Sometimes the offer of a drink may help them relax.

5. Complaints

In the best run business, mistakes are made from time to time and even when everyone is well trained in customer care there will be times when customers make complaints. Many sales people get that sinking feeling when they see customers walking towards them with tell-tale packages under their arms. This often spells out "customer return" and, sometimes, "complaint". This reaction is somewhat unfortunate, for a positive reaction to a complaint will often help to defuse it and give the business the opportunity to put things right in such a way as to befriend the customer for life.

Be positive!

Have you ever overheard this kind of conversation in a bus queue or in a pub?

"We are going out to dinner tonight but are unsure where to go. Where would you recommend, Sharon?"

"That's difficult round here. We always eat in town since that food poisoning scare last year. The trouble is the pub is very noisy and the service is slow; the bistro is pleasant enough and the food is good – Brian just reckons the portions are pathetic! I think that the Mirage Restaurant is as good as any. Mind you, the last time we ate there Brian swore he would never go there again as his meal was cold. And the prices there are just silly!"

Why didn't Brian complain at the time? At least the restaurant manager would have had the opportunity to put the problem right and might have avoided Sharon spreading the complaint all the way down the bus queue.

 Key Learning Point: The complaining customer gives us a chance to put the problem right and, if we use our customer care skills properly, we should be able to cement the customer for life.

A positive sequence

Customers who feel they have to return and make a complaint have usually rehearsed what they are going to say as they expect a tussle with your business. This is probably because they have had some bad experience with another business when making a complaint in the past rather than through their desire to avoid taking the blame themselves (only a very small minority of customers are intrinsically dishonest!). So, the immediate impact of a complaint can be defused easily by the way in which the customer is treated right at the beginning.

First of all, you should know the limits of your authority when it comes to handling complaints. If they can only be handled, practically, by your manager then it will save a great deal of time and energy if you explain this to the customer right at the start, and call the manager. This step can be carried out with tact – or by contributing to the problem! For example:

Customer: "I bought this blouse here last week and it shrank in the wash. It is disgraceful considering the price I paid for it!"

Sales Person: "You'll have to see the Buyer about it. She isn't here at the moment but will be back from lunch at 2.30 pm."

Customer: "Well can't *you* deal with it? A cash refund is quite simple, isn't it?"

Sales Person: "I'm not allowed to. I'm only a sales assistant – they don't trust people like me to handle refunds."

Customer: "Well! That means I've had a wasted journey. I can't possibly wait until 2.30 pm – I have a very important appointment."

It is not that the sales person has actually created the complaint or actually been rude. It is more likely that through her failure to sympathise with the customer the situation has not been defused and the customer will go away even more cross than she was before.

Assignment

How would you have handled this customer? Write your answer out here:

Customer: "I bought this blouse here last week and it shrank in the wash. It is disgraceful considering the price I paid for it!"

Sales Person: "You'll have to see the Buyer about it. She isn't here at the moment but will be back from lunch at 2.30 pm."

Customer: "Well can't *you* deal with it? A cash refund is quite simple, isn't it?"

Sales Person:

✍...

....

....

Apologise

The first step in defusing a customer complaint is to apologise for the inconvenience that the customer has suffered. This does not mean that you should take responsibility for what has actually gone wrong – who knows, the customer may have misused or abused the product. However, a brief apology recognises that the customer has a problem and that the business would prefer that it had not happened this way.

Obtain help

If you are unable to deal with the complaint yourself, ask a colleague – or your manager – to see the customer. Remember, the customer has probably "rehearsed the story" and will become even more angry if he or she has to repeat it to several different people.

Seat the customer

It will also help if it is possible to provide a seat for customers while they are waiting – and, even better, if this can be located in a quiet corner of the shop or department. It is difficult for the customer to be angry when sitting down and the "quiet corner" should ensure that other customers are not disturbed by an angry or embarrassing scene.

Listen and grasp the facts

Before answering any of the comments the customer might make, it is important to listen carefully to the whole story. This means trying to avoid getting emotionally involved, even though the customer may be quite provocative or possibly rude about the product, your business or the person who served them. If it is impossible for a manager to see the customer then the sales person should explain this gently and offer to take down the details – together with the customer's name and address. If you are unsure you understand any part of the story, you should ask questions and try to clarify what happened.

Take action

Customers may show more anger at staff members who do not show confidence in actioning a complaint. So, the first step is to take some notes as the story unfolds. This should convey a "business-like" approach to handling the situation and give the feeling that the firm is taking the problem seriously.

Many customers will immediately tell you what they want to happen. For example: "I think you should refund my money!" Others may be quite unsure or non-assertive about the position – even, perhaps, disappointed and hurt that they have had something go wrong. It is important not to jump to any conclusions here but to try, gently, to find out how the customer would like to see the situation resolved. A tactful question might be:

"How do you feel the problem should be resolved?"

This sounds much better than "What do you want *me* to do about it?"

Establishing blame

When you feel that the customer is in the wrong, it is best not to make this accusation. A low-key way out is to say:

"It sounds as if there has been a misunderstanding about the washing instructions." This is less provocative than: "You obviously washed this wrongly!"

Clearly, a business cannot afford to refund or credit a large proportion of its sales and, in any case, it should not carry the responsibility for substandard merchandise. So, grasping the facts about the complaint is very important if the item is to be returned to the supplier with a request for a full credit. Faulty stock should obviously be credited and the supplier, while not actually welcoming the return, should be pleased to know about any difficulties or complaints so that confidence can be rebuilt in the brand.

Maintaining loyalty

Customers are not impressed by staff who try to distance themselves from the policies of the firm. It is easy to show anger about your firm – and its suppliers – when you are on the receiving end of all the complaints. However, it does not help your business image if you respond to the complaint by attacking your firm's buying policies and say that you are "fed up with this recurring problem". Such an outburst may well contribute to the final destruction of your trading reputation.

> *Key Learning Point: Obviously, no one wishes to have to deal with complaints and unhappy people, and the records of complaints should be analysed carefully to see what corrective action can be taken to avoid the problem recurring.*

6. Questionnaire

	1	2	3	4
1. A customer arrives in your shop or department just when you are in the middle of an important stock check. Should you:				
(a) break off immediately and return to the stock check after serving	☐	☐	☐	☐
(b) ignore the customer until you reach a convenient moment to break off	☐	☐	☐	☐
(c) apologise to the customer for the delay and continue with the stock check	☐	☐	☐	☐
(d) call for your manager to serve the customer.	☐	☐	☐	☐

2. A complaining customer should be:
(a) given the Head Office address ☐ ☐ ☐ ☐
(b) offered an immediate apology and the promise of instant
    satisfaction ☐ ☐ ☐ ☐
(c) seated in a quiet corner and listened to carefully ☐ ☐ ☐ ☐
(d) corrected promptly when there appears to be an error in
    the "story". ☐ ☐ ☐ ☐

3. When offering a special order service, the customer asks
    how long deliveries will be. The experienced assistant will:
(a) promise an optimistic delivery time ☐ ☐ ☐ ☐
(b) under-promise in the expectation of improving on the
    quoted time ☐ ☐ ☐ ☐
(c) avoid any commitment ☐ ☐ ☐ ☐
(d) check with the manager. ☐ ☐ ☐ ☐

4. Customer awareness means:
(a) recognising customers in the business ☐ ☐ ☐ ☐
(b) greeting all customers as they arrive ☐ ☐ ☐ ☐
(c) putting the customer's needs first ☐ ☐ ☐ ☐
(d) presenting yourself with friendliness and professionalism. ☐ ☐ ☐ ☐

5. Customers who telephone in at a very busy time (e.g.
    lunchtime) should be:
(a) dealt with quickly so that they do not distract you from
    serving actual customers ☐ ☐ ☐ ☐
(b) ignored until you have cleared the customers in the
    business ☐ ☐ ☐ ☐
(c) asked to call back at a quieter time ☐ ☐ ☐ ☐
(d) asked to leave their telephone number so that they can be
    called back later. ☐ ☐ ☐ ☐

Summary of Key Learning Points

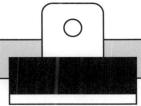

1. *Customers expect some recognition from retail staff – regardless of who they are. A simple smile and 'hello' may help to encourage customers to express their interests or needs even if you are just passing by. This may be a cue for you to find the right person to help if that is not you.*

2. *Customers must come first – all the time. This sometimes means putting ourselves out for them when it is most inconvenient, or when we feel least up to it.*

3. *The combination of 'willingness' and 'time to reflect' will sometimes encourage customers to choose from the options you have, rather than the 'impossible' choice that they were seeking.*

4. *It should not matter who makes the sale – providing that a sale is made.*

5. *Customers often measure their satisfaction by considering the number of things which go wrong in their deaings with your business. Total customer care means that everything should be right – first time.*

6. *Be polite at all times – try to maintain a professional image throughout.*

7. *Successful sales people keep in touch with customers – at all times.*

8. *Customer care techniques must extend to telephone contact with customers. Standards should be agreed with all phone users and then monitored and assessed.*

9. *Don't make promises that you (or someone else) cannot keep. Always consult the delivery service to negotiate a 'special delivery' before telling the customer.*

10. *Try to ensure that your delivery service is helped to complete the sale by delivering the customer's purchases – first time and in full.*

11. *Visitors to customers' homes must always remember that they are guests of the customer and ambassadors of their firms, and behave accordingly.*

12. *Selling is often a process of encouraging the customer to buy dreams – the 'remodelled dining-room', the 'luxury bathroom', the 'working kitchen'. The installation process must ensure that the customer's dreams come true.*

13. *Customers may prefer to choose the location for the completion of credit paperwork. Sometimes the offer of a drink may help them to relax.*

14. *The complaining customer gives us a chance to put the problem right and, if we use our customer care skills properly, we should be able to cement the customer for life.*

15. *No one wishes to have to deal with complaints and unhappy people, and the records of complaints should be analysed carefully to see what corrective action can be taken to avoid the problem recurring.*

10

How Would You Like To Pay?

"Customers enjoy a wide range of methods of payment. Our job is to ensure that the sale is processed efficiently and with style."

1. Introduction

After all the efforts to make the sale that we have described in this book it would seem to be unnecessary to discuss the completion of the sale by taking the money from the customer. However, there are still obstacles for us to negotiate if the customer is to be completely satisfied and the sale finished off efficiently.

We have probably all had second thoughts about a purchase just as we have moved to the checkout or pay desk and the reality of having to part with the money suddenly sank in. The product itself will clearly meet the needs which have been discussed with the sales person. However, new images may come to the front of the mind now that the actual payment has to be transacted. Suddenly the customer may feel petulant, manipulated, even "conned". This reaction may be directed as much against his or her partner – who may have talked him or her into the sale and left a strong feeling that little choice was possible. Such strong emotions may then be addressed to the sales person rather than to the partner and may take some strange forms.

For example, the customer may ask if a particular credit card is accepted by the store:

Customer: "Do you accept the Breakfast Club card?"
Assistant: "No, I'm afraid not."
Customer: "What? I thought everyone accepted that card! What kind of store

is this if it doesn't take the BC card? Don't you normally attract Top People then?"

Assistant: "Would you like to come across to the service desk where I am sure we can sort it out."

This suggestion is probably sufficient to encourage the customer to believe that he or she is in the hands of someone who knows how to put the customer's mind at rest and will complete the sale with a warm feeling about the purchase and the opportunity to come back sometime soon.

How do we achieve this with such discriminating customers – as well as all the others? Put simply, we do it by demonstrating our efficiency and good customer care skills in completing the sale.

In this chapter we shall examine the facilities of accepting payment of all kinds and how our competence will make all the difference in giving confidence to customers that they have made the right decision in spending their money with us.

2. Staffing the Pay Point

Some businesses expect the sales person to follow the sale right through to the point of payment. Others separate the payment process and pass this over to an administrative team whose role it is to complete the transaction.

For best effect, the transition should appear totally "seamless" (whether the ultimate transaction is undertaken by the sales person or by the cashpoint staff). The customer should not be given the impression that there will be any obstacles to a smooth transition through the sale and out into the real world. Amongst other factors this means ensuring that the customer is not obliged to wait for the cash point staff to be free to complete the transaction. Timing is of the essence and may mean delaying a coffee break if there are lots of customers about and you do not want to risk them "cooling off".

 Key Learning Point: There can be little that is more irritating for customers than to have to wait in a queue to pay for a purchase after making the decision. It will seem worse if there are unmanned stations alongside. Excellent customer care will not be achieved in such situations.

Case History

The late Sir Charles Clore, Chairman of the giant Sears retail group, set an important standard for the training of all new staff – especially in his flagship department store, Selfridges. He insisted that even if they were unable to perform any other task, everyone must be able to accept payment from customers and process the sale. At the time, this involved 26 different methods of transacting the sale and meant that all new joiners had to be given some two-and-a-half days' training so that everyone achieved full competence with the company's systems. The quotation attributed to the great entrepreneur was: "If there are customers walking around the aisles waving pound notes in the air, I want every staff member to be able to complete those sales!"

The advent of computer terminals has not changed this priority – but, as customers, we might doubt whether this standard applies in all retail businesses when we witness the skills at many service desks or cash points.

Maintaining excellent service can involve much more than just speaking persuasively to customers. It also involves putting the customer's needs first: how often have you noticed customers wanting to pay at the pay desk or walking around the sales floor waving money in the air? And, if so, were you able to act like the "fire brigade" and help the customer(s) spend their money?

Key Learning Point: An obvious priority is to ensure that processing the sale is as efficiently completed as the earlier stages.

3. The Stock Check

At the point of payment, the sales person has the last opportunity to check the merchandise with the customer – that its size, colour or quantity is correct. This apparently trivial task provides an important method of reducing mistakes which could otherwise lead to a credit or refund in a day or two. Simply reading the details on the label out loud should be sufficient for the customer to be sure that the product chosen meets the purpose intended. It is also a good time to draw the customer's attention to any washing or maintenance instructions. In addition it is the point when any stock control routines should be remembered, by maybe removing the stock ticket or recording a product code so that a replacement item may be ordered if this is needed.

Key Learning Point: The skilled sales person always looks ahead and tries to remember that the sale is just one part of the overall retailing process.

4. Payment Methods

It is normally assumed that customers should have the right to pay for their purchases in whichever way most suits them. However, *your* business may not accept every type of payment and some methods may be much more attractive to the retailer than others. This is not to say that we might actually refuse a method of payment when a customer wants to use it – but there is no harm in inviting the customer to pay, say, by cash if your firm prefers to use that method. To illustrate this point, try the following assignment.

Assignment: Types of payment compared

To complete this assignment you will probably need to obtain further information about each payment method from your manager. The surprising fact is that all payment methods actually cost the firm money to process into the bank – and some rather more than others.

Type of payment	Advantages/disadvantage to retailer	Advantages/disadvantages to customer
e.g. Cash	Instant credit in bank account Expensive in bank charges	Universal acceptance Bulky to carry in large quantities

 Key Learning Point: When customers are undecided which payment method to use, there may be one which is preferred by your firm and this might be the one to recommend.

5. Cash or Cheque?

Efficiency in cash handling should cover the following points:

- Recognition of currency. It is easy to make mistakes in accepting notes and coins – for example: are Scottish notes acceptable tender? can we accept coins from the Channel Islands, Isle of Man, or Ireland? can we recognise forged notes? and coins?
- Location of currency. Mistakes in change-giving often occur through mislocating coins and notes; failing to rest notes tendered on the cash register ledge while computing the correct change; locating notes into the wrong compartment of the drawer.
- Change computation. Even if the machine does this for you, it is sensible to build up the coins and notes as you take the change from the till. The idea of the subsequent count-back into the customer's hand is to double-check that the first change computation was correct.

Cheques also require careful handling:

- Do the figures and words match?
- Is the date correct?

- Was the cheque signed in your presence?
- Is the payee title correct?
- Do the signatures on the cheque and card match?
- Do the sort codes on the card and cheque agree?
- Is the card still valid? Has the expiry date passed?
- Is the signature panel raised (i.e. undamaged)
- Is the cheque card valid for the amount of the cheque?

Genuine mistakes happen, but the sales person must be constantly vigilant against the possibilities of:

- Stolen cheque-books and cards
- Fraud
- Forged notes and coins.

Case History

BAA operates most major airports in the UK and, at each one, duty-free shopping facilities are provided. This is now a multi-million pound operation and the shopping centres especially at Heathrow Airport rival those in many of the country's largest city high streets. Alpha Retail operates the duty-free supermarket at Terminal 1, for example, and this was completely rebuilt in 1995 to achieve a substantial increase in throughput of customers and a 20 per cent time reduction for each transaction. Delays at checkouts could cause passengers to miss their flights! Retail staff and their supervisors helped design the checkouts which were increased in number by 10 per cent. New customer care standards were introduced with staff enabled to accept payment – and give change – in 20 different currencies and accept six different credit cards.

---

6. Paying by Credit Card or House Account

When credit cards were first launched in the UK they were advertised as a way of "taking the waiting out of wanting" – and that is precisely what they do. In fact, they do it so well that some people may be tempted to spend rather more money on their accounts than they can really afford. This is why all card transactions above a prearranged "floor limit" normally must be sanctioned either via the electronic transmission system (PDQ machine) or by telephone call.

Once again there are strengths and weaknesses in accepting credit cards.

The main disadvantage from the retailer's viewpoint lies in the commission rate which is charged by the banks. It could be argued that this is a small price to pay for guaranteed credit but, given the popularity of plastic cards and increased pressure on profit margins, retailers might be forgiven for wanting to negotiate with the banks to minimise the commission rate.

Credit cards are also very popular targets for thieves, which means that stolen cards are sometimes presented in shops for the payment of goods. This apparently uncontrollable risk can bring an unexpected bonus when the card company provides a reward for the person who is able to confiscate the card of a person who has overspent their limit or is using a stolen card. (A more difficult matter is how to handle angry customers who have the unpleasant experience of watching their cards being destroyed in front of their eyes!)

Credit cards and cheques provide an additional advantage over cash: they reveal the customer's name and this enables the sales person to personalise the final conversation before the customer finally leaves the business – a nice touch which can cement relationships when a sincere approach is used.

House accounts (either monthly or deferred payment terms) can provide the same kind of facility as bank cards, the main advantage to the retailer being that the account system is seen by the customer as being the retailer's own "house" account system. Obviously, with ownership comes responsibility and the costs of operating such a credit system must also be met; however, an extensive debtor list can provide a good route to a client mailing list because it gives clear access to customers' buying habits and their likelihood of meeting their bills. Many account systems require the retailer to obtain internal sanction for expenditure above a certain limit, mainly as a precaution that a customer does not overspend.

 Key Learning Point: Credit card vouchers are just as valuable to the business as cash. They must be protected in exactly the same ways as cash.

7. Registering the Sale and Giving Change

Cash-point equipment has become significantly more sophisticated in the last decade as computer systems have begun to take over more of the retailing functions which were previously undertaken manually. For example, electronic point of sale systems (EPOS) make automatic updating of stock records a reality with little involvement of the sales person. Laser readers even save the process of keying in the stock code for each item sold.

So, what distinguishes effective cash-point service from the "average treatment" which may be meted out to customers in some shops?

- The sales person can operate the equipment correctly – first time.
- If an error does occur, the sales person knows how to correct it with no delay.
- The customer's needs are met first – and administrative systems are a close second.
- The cash till is well provisioned with spare till rolls and audit rolls and the staff can replace them when the need arises.
- All the sales team observe the firm's security procedures for the correct handling of cash and the till is kept locked when it is not in use.
- Any safety problems at the cash point are identified, quickly reported and rectified (e.g. dangerous cables, broken glass, sharp edges)
- Packing materials are kept in stock at the cash point and the sales staff can select appropriate-sized bags and materials for the purchases involved.
- All staff can identify and process alternative non-cash items tendered by customers, such as credit notes, gift tokens, promotion coupons, etc.

Quite often the sales person has to give change and, again, staff at the effective service point will take much more trouble than those in other businesses. Counting back change should be a simple and logical task but it is surprising how often we are given the wrong change in shops. The answer is to add up the change from the till into your own hand and then cross-check it by counting the change back into the customer's hand. This means that the customer can check the change as the sales person hands it over. (Some businesses have used signs by the cash point which instruct the customer to "Check your change – mistakes cannot be rectified afterwards". If correct and efficient procedures were used in the first place, such signs would not be needed.).

 Key Learning Point: Good systems and procedures – carried out by well trained staff – will ensure that mistakes are not made and that the customer is impressed by your efficiency.

8. Valuing the Purchase by Special Wrapping

The final service step for the customer's purchase is the packaging. The speed of service in many cash-and-wrap sales demands a quick placing of the merchandise into a simple bag so that the customer is not delayed unneces-sarily. However, this mentality has rather eclipsed the idea that the purchase should be packaged in a way which is compatible with its value. This could mean making a parcel out of gift wrap (in the case of a small, boxed item) or carefully protecting a garment from creasing (using tissue paper before the item is placed into a carrier bag). It is noticeable that this packaging care is more frequently offered in Europe than in the UK although it is worth noting that specialist retailers tend to be more service-oriented in this field.

 Key Learning Point: Good service impact can be gained from giving the customer's purchase an equivalent level of care and value in the packaging.

9. The Receipt

Many sales people give little thought to the value of the sales receipt – that is, until the customer decides to bring the purchase back. The till receipt may seem to be unimportant but it provides proof of purchase for the customer, which may be more important than we expect. Apart from acting as a record of the sale, the receipt proves that the product was actually bought – which may be important if the customer is obliged to prove that he or she was not involved in shoplifting!

So, if the receipt is important it should be treated as such when the sale is transacted. Many sales people toss the till slip into the bag with the purchase where it is probably lost when the purchase is unpacked or when the bag is thrown away. A better way is for the receipt to be handed to the customer, *after* passing over any change. This will usually be appreciated by the customer who may well wish to store the receipt somewhere different from the loose change. (It can be very irritating to be handed a handful of coins, maybe some notes and the receipt in the middle of it all.)

 Key Learning Point: The customer's receipt should be passed to the customer at the end of the transaction with words which endorse its importance (for example, "and there is your receipt – you might need that if you decide you want to change the item").

10. The Commendation

Finally, the sales person has the opportunity – in parting from the customer – to reinforce the positive feelings that have been built up through the sales interview. This is best done by:

- Thanking customers for their business
- Commending the purchase (e.g. "I'm sure you will be very pleased with it.")
- Saying goodbye in such a way that the customer will want to return.

In bygone times the sales person would also see the customer out and the door would be held open for the customer to leave; in some situations this is still possible and much appreciated by many customers.

 Key Learning Point: It is important that customers feel valued right up to the point where they leave the business; it conveys entirely the wrong impression if the sales person appears to "bundle the customer out of the shop" when the money is in the till.

11. Questionnaire

	1	2	3	4
1. Mistakes made by customers choosing wrong-sized goods can be avoided by:				
(a) a stock-check at the cashpoint when the customer comes to pay	☐	☐	☐	☐
(b) giving more attention to qualifying the customer	☐	☐	☐	☐
(c) ensuring all stock is correctly labelled	☐	☐	☐	☐
(d) the customer always trying a garment/shoes on.	☐	☐	☐	☐
2. Name the important item to check on credit card vouchers and cheques:				
(a) the date of the transaction	☐	☐	☐	☐
(b) the amounts matching – words and figures	☐	☐	☐	☐
(c) signature matching the customer's card	☐	☐	☐	☐
(d) amount matches the transaction value.	☐	☐	☐	☐
3. Giving the correct change is easier if:				
(a) the till calculates it for you	☐	☐	☐	☐
(b) the sales person is qualified in maths	☐	☐	☐	☐
(c) the customer has a quick brain to catch mistakes	☐	☐	☐	☐
(d) the assistant counts back the change into the customer's hand	☐	☐	☐	☐
4. The receipt is:				
(a) best placed into the bag containing the purchase	☐	☐	☐	☐
(b) an important record of the transaction	☐	☐	☐	☐
(c) the customer's record which is needed if a subsequent complaint	☐	☐	☐	☐
(d) an item of waste paper.	☐	☐	☐	☐

5. The last verbal contact with the customer should be:
(a) giving the customer the receipt
(b) a warm "goodbye"
(c) a commendation and "thank you" for the business
(d) passing over a business card to the customer.

Summary of Key Learning Points

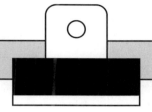

1. There can be little that is more irritating for customers than to have to wait in a queue to pay for a purchase after making the decision. It will seem worse if there are unstaffed stations alongside. Excellent customer care will not be achieved in such situations.

2. An obvious priority is to ensure that processing the sale is as efficiently completed as the earlier stages.

3. The skilled sales person always looks ahead and tries to remember that the sale is just one part of the overall retailing process.

4. When customers are undecided as to which payment method to use, there may be one which is preferred by your firm and this might be the one to recommend.

5. Credit card vouchers are just as valuable to the firm as cash. They must be protected in exactly the same way as cash.

6. Good systems and procedures – carried out by well-trained staff – will ensure that mistakes are not made and that the customer is impressed by your efficiency.

7. Good service impact can be gained by giving the customer's purchase an equivalent level of care and value in the packaging.

8. The customer's receipt should be passed to the customer at the end of the transaction with words which endorse its importance (for example,'and there is your receipt – you might need that if you decide you want to change it'.).

9. It is important that customers feel valued right up to the point that they leave the business; it conveys entirely the wrong impression if the sales person appears to bundle the customer out of the shop as soon as the money is in the till.

11

Continuing the Development Process

"I like to think that I make the most of every opportunity I have to improve my own selling skills – training, learning by example and everyday experiences all have something to teach me."

1. Introduction

For the person who is determined to be successful, selling can provide a fascinating career. As we have seen, it can be a job which involves strategy, tactics, communication techniques, body language and influencing skills – and all skilled sales people tend to develop their own selling style. No one set of techniques will bring instant and reliable success. However, with persistence, good product knowledge and an extrovert personality there is a good chance of achieving above average results. There is no reason why this should not lead to "top sales" status and reputation.

A book like this provides a valuable resource of ideas and techniques but selling is an essentially practical skill which is best developed through practical work. This last chapter gives a range of suggestions on how to keep the development process going throughout your selling career.

2. Look and Listen

There is no such thing as copyright in sales conversations and there is no reason why any sales person should not use sales lines used by colleagues in the business or, indeed, anywhere else. So, two positive steps that everyone can take in improving sales technique are:

- Listen to and watch experienced sales people in your firm as they endeavour to sell to customers. Do not be afraid to copy the approaches which are successful.
- Observe and learn from techniques used by sales people on you when you are the customer for another business's products or services. Direct sales people tend to be best at new approaches and certainly set an example for persistence; they have to be persistent or they do not make a living (especially if they are motivated by a high rate of commission).

Just one reminder, though: the easiest person to sell to is another sales person, so be careful that you are not so mesmerised by the person's technique that you lose all your sales resistance and become a "pushover".

Similarly, you may have the opportunity to witness a sales representative selling to your buyer and, again, this opportunity will provide you with more examples of what to do – and what not to do – and maybe your buyer will give you some feedback on why he or she did or did not buy. Such coaching conversations are more valuable than they seem at first sight. We are very rarely right all the time and it is easy to lose confidence in selling when business is tough and the sales just do not seem to come. These are the times when all sales people need support and the self-opinionated and "always right" person may find it doubly hard to re-examine his or her style and technique.

 Key Learning Point: Learn about alternative sales approaches by "tuning in" to sales strategies used by your (successful) colleagues and sales people who are trying to sell to you.

3. Be an Interesting Person to Talk to

One of the worst adjectives that can be applied to someone in selling is "boring". The symptoms of a boring personality are:

- The sales person has no enthusiasm
- He or she speaks in a monotone
- His or her personal presentation is "grey" and without character
- He or she has little small talk and no views on current events.

It is unlikely that any of us can compensate for an introverted personality if we are not shown and helped to correct this in selling situations (training courses can help quite a lot). However, being amongst people, interacting with them – and keeping up to date by reading – can help a great deal.

Key Learning Point: Many sales situations do not require high-level performance – only politeness and efficiency – but customers can still distinguish those who are interested in the job from those who are not.

4. Become a Self-Developer

Training is important for all sales people, but it is not the only way in which you can improve your skills. This section sets out some simple approaches to self-development.

Review your own progress

Many businesses and managers organise performance review meetings with their staff. The value of these discussions is to provide encouragement to achieve even better results in the job and they should have a real motivating effect. However, it is tempting to defend yourself if the manager has any criticisms of your work and performance. Try to resist this temptation: listen carefully and set about trying to improve. Appraisal meetings also provide opportunities to air differences, criticisms and suggestions about the business – for example, when discussing the product range. It is always better to be constructive in such discussions and resist the temptation to be negative.

The lack of an appraisal system does not mean that we cannot review our own performance from time to time. This might not be attractive because, to be effective, you should try to list your strengths *and* weaknesses as a sales person. The aim then is to concentrate on improving those weaknesses and exploiting the strengths. Quite often we find that the things we least like doing are also the tasks we are least good at and vice versa. A typical example of this could be being less enthusiastic about making sales of accessories rather than a full suit or outfit. So, it would be good to try to become excellent at selling the whole merchandise range.

 Key Learning Point: Set your sights high and your performance will improve.

Read books on selling

We have included a brief reading list in Appendix 1 and this should provide a good place to start in increasing your knowledge of selling skills. Selling is not an academic skill – but just one new idea found in a book will be worth all the effort you made to read it. As you are reading do not ask whether these are new ideas, rather you should ask: "Do I really try to put this idea into practice? And to what extent am I successful?"

Teach others

As you become more experienced at selling – and more successful – you should take an interest in helping other, less experienced, sales people. You will find that, as you teach others, so you will learn yourself.

5. Benefit from Training Opportunities

When training opportunities arise the effective sales person will embrace them enthusiastically. Experience does not mean that we cannot benefit from training but it is important to approach the training with an open mind and a determination to gain and contribute to the success of the event. For example, training workshops may give participants the opportunity to test out their skills and review the results on video – an intimidating prospect for most of us. However, all we are seeing is what everyone else is seeing! So, perhaps we should be able to use the experience to "benchmark" our skills and then set about achieving the improvement.

 Key Learning Point: We can all learn something in training sessions – even if it is something about ourselves.

6. Persuasion Skills in Life

Selling skills are useful in both business and in life. For example, buyers have to persuade their suppliers – and this may involve "selling" their position or company needs as part of a negotiation.

In other business situations, managers find themselves having to make presentations to persuade the Board to invest more money into their departments' stock, fixtures, etc., and this might require backing from the firm's bank manager. In fact, most conversations we have in business usually have some ulterior motive – to persuade someone to do something differently in some way – and this could include:

- Persuading a colleague that even though he or she might not like the latest stock delivery, customers will still buy the products.
- Seeking to persuade the buyer that the product range should be changed to meet customers' expectations and demands
- Persuading a customer to buy the product in stock rather than to request a special order for a preferred style which may be difficult and expensive to obtain.

People who possess, and can use, these persuasion skills are readily employable in all walks of life. Do you find it possible to "cross-fertilise" your skills in different parts of your life? For example, persuasion skills are valuable in family life, too – persuading your family or partner that your choice of holiday resort is best may be an uphill struggle but it could be a good test of your skills! Or maybe you would prefer to see a particular film this weekend while your partner would prefer another. Could this be another test of your "features and benefits" analysis?

 Key Learning Point: Selling skills can be practised in all walks of life. You could practise some of your selling techniques in your domestic life too. The consequences for "failing to convince the customer" may not be as serious as failing to make the sale in the shop.

7. Always Look on the Bright Side!

Retailing can be fun, hard work, challenging and highly stimulating. It can also have boring periods leading to our feeling dull and drained of energy and longing for another job. Which scenario is yours? Are you able to keep yourself busy when there are no customers about? What type of activity do you follow? Cleaning, stock work? Or word games and role plays? Your brain works better – and sharper – when it is in practice, so interactive exercises with colleagues will help you avoid those periods of boredom which might otherwise dull the brain.

Ultimately, the ability to see direct results from your work is one of the main sources of satisfaction to be gained from selling – and it is an occupation in which rewards can be directly affected by effort. Hard work is the best way to make a good impression in retailing – on both customers and managers – and your determination to succeed and improve sales results (while also impressing people with your willingness to put yourself out for them) will earn you a reputation of being an achiever. There will always be a job role for such sales people in retailing – and in other industries. Master the skills in this book and you should see your future secure and affluent. You will certainly have passed the first rungs on the success ladder and will be well on the way towards achieving a promotion role into departmental or branch management. Then a whole new set of challenges awaits you, but that is another story – one that we will address at another time.

 Key Learning Point: The ability to see direct results from your work is one of the main sources of satisfaction to be gained from selling – and it is an occupation in which rewards can be directly affected by effort.

Assignment

Here is your last opportunity to review some of the key skills described in earlier chapters. See how much you can remember.

1. List ten ways of grasping a customer's attention:

   1. ....

   2. ....

   3. ....

4. ....

5. ....

6. ....

7. ....

8. ....

9. ....

10. ....

2. List eight elements of body language which convey a customer's state of mind:

1. ....

2. ....

3. ....

4. ....

5. ....

6. ....

7. ....

8. ....

3. List five buying motives:

1. ....

2. ....

3. ....

4. ....

5. ....

4. What does CREWSADE represent?

    C = ...

    R = ...

    E =..

    W =..

    S =..

    A =..

    D = ...

    E =..

5. Name four types of customer reaction in a sales interview:

    1. ....

    2. ....

    3. ....

    4. ....

6. There are ten closing methods. What are they and when should they be used?

    1. ....

    2. ....

    3. ....

    4. ....

    5. ....

    6. ....

    7. ....

    8. ....

    9. ....

    10. ....

7. Name 4 skills needed in related selling:

   1. ....

   2. ....

   3. ....

   4. ....

8. What should be done to avoid the repetition of customer complaints?

   ....

   ....

   ....

9. How should the business ensure that customers do not have to wait unnecessarily at the cashpoint?

   ....

   ....

When you have completed these exercises check the answers in Appendix 2.

10. Now return to the exercise you tried at the start of this book ...

Inventory of personal skills

Please circle the score which reflects your current skill level – perhaps measured against a colleague whose skills and experience are superior or inferior to yours. Then place a cross against the score which represents your target skill level. Score: 1 = Undeveloped; Score 5 = Highly developed.

When you have completed this exercise you should then compare your ratings with those you entered into the chart in Chapter 1. There should be some positive changes!

	1	2	3	4	5
Presenting confidently	1	2	3	4	5
Empathy	1	2	3	4	5
Resilience in handling rejection	1	2	3	4	5
Sincerity	1	2	3	4	5
Open questions	1	2	3	4	5
Normally overcoming objections	1	2	3	4	5
Answering questions	1	2	3	4	5
Looking for buying signals	1	2	3	4	5
Selection – helping the customer choose	1	2	3	4	5
Knowledge of products	1	2	3	4	5
Integrity	1	2	3	4	5
Listening skills	1	2	3	4	5
Leading to a close	1	2	3	4	5
Selling up and selling on	1	2	3	4	5

Good luck in putting all these ideas into practice and with your future selling career.

Summary of Key Learning Points

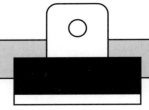

1. Learn about alternative sales approaches by 'tuning in' to sales strategies used by your (successful) colleagues and sales people who are trying to sell to you.

2. Many sales situations do not require high-level performance – only politeness and efficiency – but customers can still distinguish those who are interested in the job and those who are not.

3. Set your sights high and your performance will improve.

4. We can all learn something in training sessions – even if it is something about ourselves.

5. Selling skills can be practised in all walks of life. You could practise some of your selling techniques in your domestic life too. The consequences for failing to convince the customer may not be as serious as failing to make the sale in the shop.

6. The ability to see direct results from your work is one of the main sources of satisfaction to be gained from selling – and it is an occupation in which rewards can be directly affected by effort.

Appendix 1

Reading List

The following books will extend your knowledge of selling and interpersonal skills which will be useful for your future development. They should be available through good bookshops, your local library or direct from the publishers.

Selling Techniques

1000 Ways to Increase your Sales	Alfred Tack, Cedar Books, London
Close Close Close	John Fenton, Management Books 2000, Chalford, England
Close More Sales	Derrick White, Management Books 2000, Chalford, England
Selling... Everything You Always Wanted to Know But Were Afraid to Ask	Tony Adams, Management Books 2000, Chalford, England
Successful Retail Sales	Mills and Paul, Prentice-Hall, USA

Influencing Skills

Body Language	Allan Pease, Sheldon Press, London
How to Negotiate Better Deals	Jeremy Thorn, Management Books 2000, Chalford, England
How to Win Friends and Influence People	Dale Carnegie, Cedar, London
I'm OK – You're OK	Thomas A Harris, Pan Books Ltd., London
Negotiating the Better Deal	Peter Fleming, Routledge, London
Psychology of Interpersonal Behaviour	Michael Argyle, Pelican, England
Successful Negotiation in a Week	Peter Fleming, Hodder & Stoughton
Your Ticket to Success – NLP in Selling	Alex Macmillan, Management Books 2000, Chalford England

Appendix 2

Model Answers and Advice on Assignments

Chapter 1

Assignment 1: Handling rejection

In the three examples write in the exchange you would make to the customer/caller:

Example 1
Assistant: "Good morning."
Customer ignores the greeting and walks right past to look at something at the far end of the shop or restaurant.
Model answer: "Were you looking for something particular, sir? We have just rearranged some of our stock so you may need some directions. How can I help?"

Example 2
Assistant: "Hello, can I help you?"
Customer: "No thank you, I'm just looking."
Model answer: "Fine! Our Spring ranges are just arriving now so we have some new designs to look at. Please just ask if you would like any further information or help."

Example 3
Operator: "Thank you for calling Blands of Westhampton. Tracy speaking, how may I help you?"
Caller: "Mr Jenkins." (the name of one of your firm's managers)

Model answer: "That is Mr Jenkins in the Advertising Department?"
Caller: "Yes please."
Operator: "I'll just try to put you through now."

Assignment 2: Inventory of personal skills

This is not an easy exercise! Seeing ourselves as others see us requires quite a degree of personal insight and needs to be updated from time to time based on current experiences with customers and colleagues. This "stocktake" of your skills should have highlighted some specific targets for improvements in some of them. Especially urgent will be those for which you circled a "3" or less – but the exercise was such that all gaps between actual and target scores should provide useful training aims as you work through this book.

When you have completed the text, it would be a good idea to return to this exercise right at the end and see if improvements in your scores have been achieved.

Scoring for questionnaire (page 27)

You score one point for each correct placing:

1. (a) = 1	2. (a) = 4	3. (a) = 4	4. (a) = 4	5. (a) = 1	6. (a) = 2	7. (a) = 3	8. (a) = 3
(b) = 4	(b) = 2	(b) = 1	(b) = 3	(b) = 3	(b) = 1	(b) = 4	(b) = 1
(c) = 2	(c) = 3	(c) = 2	(c) = 1	(c) = 4	(c) = 4	(c) = 1	(c) = 2
(d) = 3	(d) = 1	(d) = 3	(d) = 2	(d) = 2	(d) = 3	(d) = 2	(d) = 4

Your total .... in Chapter 1 – out of 32 points

Chapter 2

Model Answers: Attraction factors

Colour
Seasonality
Promotion
Price (i.e. a bargain)
Volume of stock (a lot or a little)
Attractive mannequins/fixturing
Merchandise collection
Lighting
Graphics

Factors which influence customers to buy

Accessibility to merchandise by customers

Activity levels in the business (and levels of urgency)

Condition of air (fresh/stale, smells, etc.)

Atmosphere

Attention (the way the customer's attention is grasped)

Cleanliness

Company policy (on such matters as prompt greeting of visitors, stock presentation, etc.)

Decor

Displays (i.e. attempts to create an inspirational atmosphere)

Layout (e.g. walkways, location of stock and payment points)

Lighting

Merchandise itself

Noise (e.g. music, volume of conversation, etc.)

People (e.g. presentable, offputting, charming/aggressive, etc.)

Pricing – discreet and up-market, aggressive and promotional?

Space around fixtures

(Merchandise or fittings can be too crowded giving the feeling that customers' needs have not been considered)

Temperature

Tidiness

Way the shelves are stocked and laid out.

Scoring for questionnaire (page 39)

You score one point for each correct placing:

1. (a) = 3	2. (a) = 2	3. (a) = 1	4. (a) = 3	5. (a) = 4	6. (a) = 1	7. (a) = 3	8. (a) = 1
(b) = 4	(b) = 1	(b) = 2	(b) = 2	(b) = 3	(b) = 3	(b) = 4	(b) = 4
(c) = 1	(c) = 4	(c) = 3	(c) = 4	(c) = 2	(c) = 2	(c) = 2	(c) = 2
(d) = 2	(d) = 3	(d) = 4	(d) = 1	(d) = 1	(d) = 4	(d) = 1	(d) = 3

Your total .... in Chapter 2 – out of 32 points

Chapter 3

Assignment 1

What could the following signals mean and how should the sales person react?

(a)	Signals	Your Action
	Rushed movements	Prompt approach to customer
	Frequent glances at the watch	Concern about car parking/bus times, etc.
	Hurried search through stock	Mental preparation of stock position
(b)	Pursed lips	Prepare for a tense customer
	"Tutting" while waiting	Prepare a calming apology for the delay
	Clutching a package tightly	Expect a returned item and that a manager might be needed
	Furrowed brow	Impress your customer with your sympathy and listening skills

Assignment 2

You were asked to consider the following signals and how you would "read" them, and what action you would take:

Signal	Possible meaning	Action
1. Finger touching lips	Thinking or unsure what to choose	Offer advice or help
2. Hand rubbing back of neck	Tension/concern/worry	Offer advice or help
3. Hand brushes across forehead	Hot or tense	Give customer "space"
4. Hand rubbing nose	Uncomfortable – maybe with something they or you are saying	Take care. Listen carefully
5. Finger stretching/easing collar	As above	As above
6. Hand holding chin	Thinking or listening	Use check questions to see what progress you are making

Scoring for questionnaire (page 55)

You score one point for each correct placing:

1.	2.	3.	4.	5.	6.	7	8
(a) = 4	(a) = 2	(a) = 3	(a) = 4	(a) = 1	(a) = 1	(a) = 2	(a) = 4
(b) = 2	(b) = 4	(b) = 2	(b) = 1	(b) = 2	(b) = 2	(b) = 3	(b) = 2
(c) = 3	(c) = 1	(c) = 1	(c) = 2	(c) = 4	(c) = 3	(c) = 1	(c) = 1
(d) = 1	(d) = 3	(d) = 4	(d) = 3	(d) = 3	(d) = 4	(d) = 4	(d) = 4

Your total .... in Chapter 3 – out of 32 points

Chapter 4

Assignment 1

This assignment is best checked by your supervisor or manager.

Assignment 2

Examples of questions to use ....

1. WHAT kind of car did you have in mind?
2. HOW much use will you be making of it?
3. WHERE are you intending to go?
4. HOW many of you will be travelling?
5. WHY not consider a "people mover"?
6. WHEN are you intending to make this journey?

Scoring for questionnaire on page 74

1.	2.	3.	4.	5.	6.
(a) = 4	(a) = 2	(a) = 2	(a) = 1	(a) = 3	(a) = 3
(b) = 4	(b) = 4	(b) = 1	(b) = 4	(b) = 2	(b) = 2
(c) = 1	(c) = 3	(c) = 4	(c) = 3	(c) = 1	(c) = 4
(d) = 2	(d) = 1	(d) = 4	(d) = 2	(d) = 4	(d) = 1

Your total .... in Chapter 4 – out of 24 points

Chapter 5

Assignments 1, 2, 3 and 4

These are best checked by your supervisor or manager. What are you doing about any gaps in your product knowledge, by the way?

Chapter 6

Assignment 1
This task should be discussed with your colleagues or friends. How do they feel and behave when they go shopping? Are these reactions similar to any of those from your study?

Assignment 2

		Category
(i)	Do you have this in other colours?	A
(ii)	Can I change it if it is wrong when I get it home?	A
(iii)	Is it washable?	A
(iv)	How do these wear?	A/C
(v)	Will this be comfortable in the sunshine?	A/C
(vi)	How warm will this be in winter?	A/C
(vii)	Is this quality suitable for my stairs?	A/C
(viii)	Didn't I see this advertised at a lower price recently?	A/C
(ix)	I'm sure that my aunt had one of these and the corner joints came apart.	B
(x)	I really don't like these foreign made products. Do they really wear well?	D/A
(xi)	You hear a lot about poor safety with electrical goods. Are these really safe?	C/A
(xii)	How long is the guarantee? What happens afterwards?	A/A
(xiii)	Have you sold many of these? I don't want to walk into it wherever I go!	A/B
(xiv)	This doesn't look as good as it does in the window	B/D

Scoring for questionnaire (page 107)
You score one point for every correct placing:

1.	(a) = 2	2.	(a) = 4	3.	(a) = 2	4.	(a) = 2
	(b) = 4		(b) = 2		(b) = 3		(b) = 3
	(c) = 1		(c) = 3		(c) = 1		(c) = 1
	(d) = 4		(d) = 1		(d) = 4		(d) = 4

Your total .... in Chapter 6 – out of 24 points

Chapter 7

Scoring for questionnaire (page 120)

1.(a) = 3	2.(a) = 2	3.(a) = 1	4.(a) = 2	5.(a) = 3
(b) = 1	(b) = 3	(b) = 1	(b) = 1	(b) = 1
(c) = 4	(c) = 1	(c) = 4	(c) = 4	(c) = 4
(d) = 2	(d) = 4	(d) = 3	(d) = 3	(d) = 2

Your total .... in Chapter 7 – out of 20 points

Chapter 8

Scoring for questionnaire (page 133)

1.(a) = 2	2.(a) = 3	3.(a) = 3	4.(a) = 3	5.(a) = 1	6.(a) = 4
(b) = 4	(b) = 2	(b) = 2	(b) = 1	(b) = 4	(b) = 3
(c) = 2	(c) = 1	(c) = 1	(c) = 1	(c) = 2	(c) = 1
(d) = 1	(d) = 4	(d) = 4	(d) = 4	(d) = 3	(d) = 2

Your total .... in Chapter 8 – out of 24 points

Chapter 9

Assignment
Write your answer out here:

1. Customer: "I bought this blouse here last week and it shrank in the wash. It is disgraceful considering the price I paid for it!"
2. Sales Person: "You'll have to see the Buyer about it. She isn't here at the moment but will be back from lunch at 2.30 pm."
3. Customer: "Well, can't *you* deal with it? A cash refund is quite simple, isn't it?"
4. Sales Person: "I'm very sorry you have had this problem. I'm afraid that our buyer is away at the moment but perhaps you would like to talk to the department manager? Could you just give me your name and I will fetch her."

Scoring for questionnaire (page 151)

1.(a) = 1	2.(a) = 3	3.(a) = 4	4.(a) = 4	5.(a) = 1
(b) = 4	(b) = 2	(b) = 1	(b) = 1	(b) = 4
(c) = 4	(c) = 1	(c) = 4	(c) = 2	(c) = 4
(d) = 2	(d) = 4	(d) = 2	(d) = 3	(d) = 2

Your total .... in Chapter 9 – out of 20 points

Chapter 10

Assignment
You will need to check your answers with your manager.

Scoring for questionnaire (page 163)

1.(a) = 1	2.(a) = 3	3.(a) = 2	4.(a) = 3	5.(a) = 3
(b) = 3	(b) = 4	(b) = 4	(b) = 2	(b) = 2
(c) = 4	(c) = 1	(c) = 4	(c) = 1	(c) = 1
(d) = 2	(d) = 2	(d) = 1	(d) = 4	(d) = 4

Your total .... in Chapter 10 – out of 20 points

Chapter 11

Assignment
Question 1: Ten ways of grasping a customer's attention are listed in Chapter 2.
Question 2: Eight elements of body language are listed in Chapter 3.
Question 3: Five buying motives are listed in Chapter 4.
Question 4: CREWSADE is described in Chapter 5.
Question 5: Four types of customer reaction are described in Chapter 6.
Question 6: Ten closing methods are described in Chapter 7.
Question 7: Four skills needed in related selling are described in Chapter 8.
Question 8: Repetition of customer complaints will be avoided through Key Learning Point 15 in Chapter 9.
Question 9: See section 2 in Chapter 10.

BSSA Training Programme

The British Shops and Stores Association produces an annual training programme with the sole aim of developing the competence and skills of retail staff and proprietors, particularly where selling, buying, and management is concerned. Many of these programmes complement the contents of this book; however, those listed below will be of particular relevance.

Selling – Everyone's Business Workshop

This is the practical seminar related to this book. When business is difficult, every opportunity to impress the customer needs to be seized!

This fast-moving **one-day seminar** covering the psychology of selling and the basic skills involved, will give a valuable boost to the team. Anyone with little or no formal sales training, or more experienced sales staff requiring a review of their skills, will benefit.

After the workshop, delegates will be able to use a structured approach to customer service; identify the five buying stages; use persuasive vocabulary to encourage buying; sell the benefits of merchandise, and close the sale.

For those pursuing a career in specialist sales, two further **open learning programmes** are available which follow on from the Retail Selling Course. They are the **Certificate in Menswear** and the **Certificate in Womenswear.** Both lay important product knowledge foundations which will help salespeople develop their confidence in presenting merchandise to discriminating customers. The result is in-depth knowledge of fibres, fabrics, and speciality materials which will enhance sales.

Advanced Selling and Customer Care Workshop

This two-day **development workshop** provides an opportunity for more experienced sales staff to review their skills against a challenging programme. Significant improvements in performance on the sales floor will result. Beneficiaries include sales staff with at least one year's experience - or those that have already participated in foundation programmes such as the Retail Selling Course.

At the end of the workshop, delegates will be able to assess and choose a balanced selling style appropriate to both the customer and the situation. Using an active merchandising environment they will also be able to increase impulse sales.

Performing as an effective player within the sales team, successful candidates will learn to handle difficult customer situations and overcome objections, close sales, and implement their own sales improvement plan.

Methods including cctv role-play exercises, group discussion, video and pen and paper tests are used to examine the psychological aspects of selling and improve the performance of each participant.

Retail Selling Course

This popular **open learning** course aims to establish a framework of work-based competence, improve the efficiency of retail staff, and add to their appreciation of the important role they play within the company.

The main beneficiaries include recently appointed sales assistants and returnees to work who require a reaffirmation of their skills - establishing knowledge of their company, customers and merchandise – before learning basic sales techniques and putting them into practice.

The course covers such vital areas as product attributes and selling points, buying motives, opening the sale and increasing sales. Preventing and dealing with objections is covered in detail, as are security and loss control, and effective use of time.

Training materials are provided in the form of a loose-leaf manual divided into six studies, each of which is followed by a case study to be completed and returned to BSSA. Designed to test understanding and indicate progress, each case study is assessed and returned to the student and this, together with the results of a final written examination, determines the award of a completion certificate and 'Sales-Trained' badge.

Details of individual programmes may be subject to change. However, further details of these courses, and others such as the Management Development School and Oxford Summer School, may be obtained from the British Shops and Stores Association, Middleton House, Main Road, Middleton Cheney, Oxon, OX17 2TN (Telephone 01295-712277 or Facsimile 01295-711665).

INDEX